The Kenai Peninsula

ALASKA GEOGRAPHIC

Volume 21, Number 2 / 1994

The Alaska Geographic Society

To teach many to better know and more wisely use our natural resources...

Editor
Penny Rennick

Production Director
Kathy Doogan

Staff Writer
L.J. Campbell

Bookkeeper/Database Manager
Vickie Staples

Marketing Manager
Pattey Parker

Postmaster: Send address changes to
ALASKA GEOGRAPHIC®
P.O. Box 93370
Anchorage, Alaska 99509-3370

PRINTED IN U.S.A.

COVER: *A hiker overlooks Kenai Lake, a 24-mile, S-shaped lake in the Kenai Mountains. (Helen Rhode)*

PREVIOUS PAGE: *Low winter clouds hug Placer River valley at the head of Turnagain Arm. The Placer River is popular in spring with hooligan fishermen, who dip the smelt with long-handled nets. The sunlit mountains divide the peninsula from western Prince William Sound. (Michael DeYoung)*

FACING PAGE: *Seth (6) and Molly (4) Perkins were a year younger when they picked poppies for this photo at their home at Halibut Cove. Their father, Dan, does carpentry work and operates a sawmill; their mother trains border collies for dog trials and is a part-time commercial fisherwoman. (Cross Fox Photography)*

ISBN: 1-56661-020-6

Price to non-members this issue: $19.95

ALASKA GEOGRAPHIC® is published quarterly by The Alaska Geographic Society, 639 West International Airport Road, Unit 38, Anchorage, AK 99518. Second-class postage paid at Anchorage, Alaska, and additional mailing offices. Copyright © 1994 by The Alaska Geographic Society. All rights reserved. Registered trademark: Alaska Geographic, ISSN 0361-1353; Key title Alaska Geographic.

THE ALASKA GEOGRAPHIC SOCIETY is a non-profit, educational organization dedicated to improving geographic understanding of Alaska and the North, putting geography back in the classroom and exploring new methods of teaching and learning.

SOCIETY MEMBERS receive *ALASKA GEOGRAPHIC®*, a quality publication that devotes each quarterly issue to monographic in-depth coverage of a northern geographic region or resource-oriented subject.

MEMBERSHIP in The Alaska Geographic Society costs $39 per year, $49 to non-U.S. addresses. ($31.20 of the membership fee is for a one-year subscription to *ALASKA GEOGRAPHIC®*.) Order from The Alaska Geographic Society, Box 93370, Anchorage, AK 99509-3370; phone (907) 562-0164, fax (907) 562-0479.

SUBMITTING PHOTOGRAPHS: Please write for a list of upcoming topics or other specific photo needs and a copy of our editorial guidelines. We cannot be responsible for unsolicited submissions. Submissions not accompanied by sufficient postage for return by certified mail will be returned by regular mail.

ABOUT THIS ISSUE: Thousands of people flock each year to the Kenai Peninsula, a pendant of southcentral Alaska fondly known as the Kenai. Salmon and halibut fishing, mountains, glaciers, forests and ocean coasts are conveniently linked on the Kenai by roads dotted with interesting communities. Native and Russian histories converge on the peninsula, where Alaska's first oil strike helped focus national attention on the territory's potential as the 49th state. Past issues of *ALASKA GEOGRAPHIC®* have touched on the Kenai, but we thought this vital part of southcentral Alaska deserved more in-depth coverage.

In assembling this issue, we called on Janet R. Klein for the chapter on early people. She also wrote about many of the peninsula's communities, which are presented according to their origins as Russian settlements; mining, fishing or railroad camps; or homesteading communities.

Bob Moore drew from his years as school principal in Nikolaevsk to write about life in the largest of the peninsula's Russian Old Believers villages.

Staff writer, L.J. Campbell, and editor, Penny Rennick, wrote the remainder of the text.

We thank all those who granted interviews, particularly Walt and Elsa Pedersen, Sterling; Ed and Jeff Estes,

Moose Pass; Marge Mullen and Katherine Parker, Soldotna; Foster Singleton, Seward harbormaster; and Donna Carrigan, minerals specialist, Chugach National Forest, Seward.

We thank Ann Miller, of Hope, who graciously shared some of her 31 years of experiences in that community. She reviewed the section about Hope and spent a Saturday having other townspeople review it. We appreciate her efforts and thank those she contacted for their input.

We also thank the following people who provided information and/or reviewed sections of manuscript: Dr. George West, Homer; Chris Titus, manager of Alaska State Parks on the Kenai Peninsula; Dave Athons and Terry Bendock, biologists with the Alaska Department of Fish and Game, Soldotna; Al Johnson, president of Hope Mining Co., Anchorage; Dennis Merkes, Sterling; Ann Whitmore-Painter and Glen Szymoniak, Moose Pass; Natalia Fefelov, Nikolaevsk; Ed Holsten, Chugach National Forest, Anchorage; Dan Doshier, Kenai National Wildlife Refuge, Soldotna; and Cyndy Dickson, with the Seward Chamber of Commerce.

For research assistance, we thank Pat Richardson, U.S. Army Corps of Engineers; *Anchorage Daily News* librarian Sharon Palmisano; and Diane Rathman with the Kenai Visitor's Center.

CHANGE OF ADDRESS: The post office does not automatically forward *ALASKA GEOGRAPHIC®* when you move. To ensure continuous service, please notify us six weeks before moving. Send your new address and your membership number or a mailing label from a recent issue of *ALASKA GEOGRAPHIC®* to: The Alaska Geographic Society, Box 93370, Anchorage, AK 99509-3370.

Color Separations:
GRAPHIC CHROMATICS
Printed by:
THE HART PRESS

The Library of Congress has cataloged this serial publication as follows:

Alaska Geographic. v.1-
[Anchorage, Alaska Geographic Society]
1972-
v. ill. (part col.). 23 x 31 cm.
Quarterly
Official publication of The Alaska Geographic Society.
Key title: Alaska geographic, ISSN 0361-1353.

1. Alaska—Description and travel—1959-
—Periodicals. I. Alaska Geographic Society.

F901.A266 917.98′04′505 72-92087

Library of Congress 75[79112] MARC-S

Contents

The Kenai

By Penny Rennick

It dangles south of Anchorage, squeezed between Cook Inlet on the west and Prince William Sound on the east. It is the Kenai Peninsula, known to many Alaskans simply as the Kenai. Shaped roughly like an arrowhead, the peninsula stretches about 150 miles from Point Adam at its southwestern tip to Portage on Turnagain Arm, and about 120 miles from Nikiski on Cook Inlet to the coast of Prince William Sound. The peninsula is almost an island; if not for an isthmus a little less than 10 miles long between the head of Turnagain Arm and Passage Canal on Prince William Sound, it would be.

The Kenai Mountains, topping out at Truuli Peak, 6,612 feet, protect the peninsula's eastern and southern flanks, remnants of the time when Pleistocene glaciers scoured and shaved southern Alaska. Ground moraines and stagnant ice fashioned low ridges, hills and lowlands in the peninsula's western and northern reaches. Few uplands, such as the Caribou Hills, break this gentle landscape. The Harding Icefield blankets about 720 square miles of the mountains on the south; to the east the Sargent Icefield caps the mountains fronting Prince William Sound. From the mountains flow glaciers, seaward to the heads of fiords in the severely indented coast and landward to the heads of the peninsula's largest lakes. Tustumena and Skilak

LEFT: *A tufted puffin banks for a landing on the rocky slopes of an island in the Chiswell group, off Resurrection and Aialik bays. Numerous cruise boats make the run to the Chiswells, home to Steller sea lions and a variety of seabirds. (Paul A. Souders)*

FACING PAGE: *The Seward Highway cuts through Turnagain Pass in the Kenai Mountains on the north end of the peninsula. This is part of Chugach National Forest. In summer, hikers enjoy wildflowers such as lupine and wild geranium, which bloom profusely in the open areas and along glacial streams. Winter brings deep snow, skiers and snow machiners. (Jon R. Nickles)*

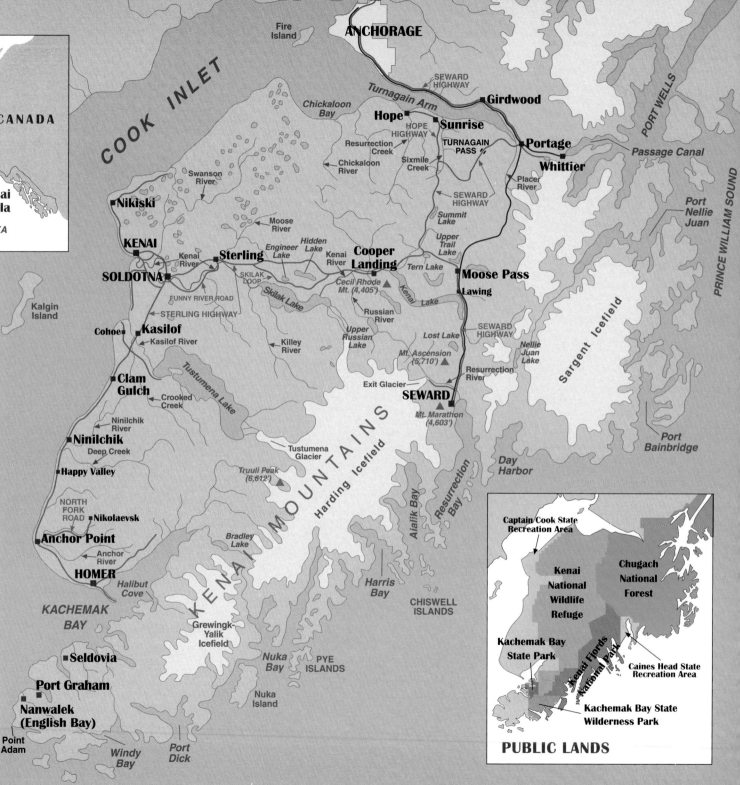

lakes, largest on the peninsula, lure fishermen and boaters, and in earlier times helped ease backcountry travel. But the lakes carry their own dangers when cold, stiff winds sweep off the glaciers.

The peninsula's climate brings temperatures that rise to 80 degrees in summer and sink to minus 30 in winter. The areas closest to the Gulf of Alaska enjoy more moderate temperatures and more precipitation; the northwestern quarter has a climate more representative of interior locations because ice cover on Cook Inlet counteracts the moderating effects of oceans on the temperature and the flat terrain provides no barriers to winds. Annual precipitation is normally 19 inches at Kenai and 25 inches at Homer. The mountainous east side receives 67 inches at Seward.

Widespread deposits of ash combine with Mesozoic-age rocks, about 250 million to 65 million years old, in the mountain flanks and Tertiary-age rocks, about 65 million to 2 million years old, in the lowlands to form the Kenai Peninsula landmass. The Mesozoic rocks are mostly mudstone and graywacke with smaller amounts of sandstone, limestone and basalt; the Tertiary rocks include siltstone, sandstone and shale. Coal beds are abundant in certain areas, and coal outcrops provide a source of fuel for coastal residents from Ninilchik south to Kachemak Bay. The Tertiary rocks underlying the lowlands are part of the Cook Inlet Sedimentary Basin, a natural reservoir whose contents would cause the drums of oil to herald visions of prosperity for the Kenai.

The biological realm of the peninsula is equally rich. From brown and black bears to tiny, fur-bearing mammals, the Kenai nourishes an abundant array of wildlife. In addition to the bears, moose and two caribou herds roam the peninsula. The lowland caribou herd is struggling, but hunters target the Kenai Mountain herd that roams in the northern mountains of the peninsula. The peninsula is one of the few places in Alaska where the ranges of Dall

Two caribou herds graze on the Kenai. A small herd roams the Kenai River flats and can sometimes be seen from the Warren Ames Bridge at Kenai. The Kenai Mountain herd ranges in the mountains of the northern peninsula. (Ron Levy)

Engineer Lake, off Skilak Lake Loop Road, is among the many lakes dotting the central peninsula's spruce, hemlock, birch and aspen forests. (Sean Reid)

sheep and mountain goats overlap. Dall sheep occur throughout the Kenai Mountains although they tend to dwindle out south of Tustumena Lake. Mountain goats, less adapted to snow, prefer the steeper, rougher terrain to the south. The lynx population on the peninsula has been under pressure for several years; wolves are taken both by sport hunters and trappers. The wolf carcasses are not eaten, instead the skins are crafted into items or are hung for display.

Bark beetles have ravaged much of the peninsula's forests. Where once great stands of healthy spruce and hemlock greeted travelers to the Kenai, acres of dead and dying forest now cover the mountainsides. Scientists from several government agencies are trying to develop a plan for dealing with the beetles. In 1994, U.S. Fish and Wildlife Service scientists were studying the history of beetle infestation on the peninsula. Teams cored trees to examine growth rings and learn when the forest canopy was thinned. This thinning allows younger trees to put on a growth spurt, and these spurts show up in the tree rings. This method provides information on the past 200 years or so; for data on earlier times, scientists plan to core lake

bottoms for beetle parts and to coordinate the cores with known ash falls, thus enabling them to get a handle on how often beetle infestations have plagued the forests.

U.S. Forest Service scientists are conducting three-pronged research into the beetle problem. They are monitoring the impacts of beetles on the ecosystem by noting the change in ground vegetation and the species and number of trees killed. The scientists have a 17-year history with these studies and have observed

Mark Norris displays his catch of razor clams dug along Cook Inlet beaches near Clam Gulch. (Helen Rhode)

The Seward Highway enters the Kenai Peninsula through the Kenai Mountains. This sole road onto the peninsula is rarely devoid of traffic, even in winter. The highway was upgraded during a several-year span in the 1980s, but narrow, winding stretches still cause bottlenecks. (Danny Daniels)

that the heavily infested forests are not regenerating with spruce and birch; instead, these areas are evolving into open, tall-grass parkland with scattered spruce, somewhat similar to the vegetation pattern around Summit Lake on the Seward Highway.

A second series of studies, ongoing for five or six years, focuses on preventive techniques: thinning and fertilizing the forest. Foresters reduce the number of trees on a plot, enabling more nutrients, sunlight and water to reach the survivors. They also add fertilizer to these plots to strengthen the remaining trees. So far, these studies have shown that the beetles are not building up as rapidly in the treated plots as they are elsewhere.

A third research emphasis investigates the chemical ecology of the bark beetles and the chemical relationship between the insects and the trees. This research involves pheromones, chemical compounds produced by the beetles to communicate. One group of pheromones attracts beetles to a tree that they want to attack and kill. A second group of pheromones repels the beetles when too many of the insects have gathered on an individual tree. Scientists hope their studies will enable them to develop compounds to trick the beetles into reacting as if a tree already had reached maximum beetle density. Preliminary results have shown that only 3 percent of trees were attacked by the beetles when these compounds were used; untreated plots suffered a 30 percent attack ratio.

According to Ed Holsten of the U.S. Forest Service's Pacific Northwest Research Station and State and

Private Forestry Branch, the bark beetles have had a huge impact on Alaska's boreal forest ecosystem including that on the Kenai. By 1993 the beetles had infested a million acres, and if mild spring weather continues in coming years, the forests will face an even greater onslaught.

Winding among these forests are the peninsula's rivers, the Kenai, Kasilof, Anchor, Resurrection and more. In many way the rivers are the essence of the Kenai, tying together east and west, interior and coastal. These waterways reflect the past, as transportation corridors and sources of food, and herald the future, as linchpins in an expanding recreation and tourist industry. This reputation as a sportsmen's paradise is tarnished a bit occasionally, when the big fish runs come in and hordes of fishermen gather. This frenzy does little, however, to diminish the overall impression of beauty and vitality associated with the Kenai Peninsula.

LEFT: *Moss and ferns cover this stairway up the steep slopes of Outer Island, seawardmost of the Pye Islands. The Pyes guard the entrance to Nuka Bay on the peninsula's outer coast. (Don Cornelius)*

ABOVE: *Boats assigned to combat the* Exxon Valdez *oil spill of 1989 patrol Windy Bay on the peninsula's outer coast. After soiling many beaches in Prince William Sound, oil from the spill was carried southwest by the currents. The oil washed into many bays along the outer coast, and reached the Barren Islands near the mouth of Cook Inlet 19 days after the spill. Some oil made its way into Cook Inlet and was spotted off Homer and Anchor Point. But many of the wildlife-rich estuaries and beaches of Kachemak Bay were spared. (Stuart Pechek)*

Prehistoric People of the Kenai Peninsula

By Janet R. Klein

Editor's note: *A resident of Homer, Janet has participated in several archaeological digs around Kachemak Bay.*

Deep in the Kenai Mountains, on a forested terrace near the confluence of the Russian and Kenai rivers, is the oldest known prehistoric site on the peninsula. About 8,000 years ago, people migrated into the narrow, glaciated river valley and found an abundance of food: salmon, snowshoe hare, sheep, beaver, bear, marmot and mountain goat.

Archaeologists excavating the Cooper Landing site in the mid-1980s unearthed unique tools called cores and microblades. These ancient artifacts are similar in style to ones found in 8,000- to 10,000-year-old sites elsewhere in Alaska. Precisely how the finely crafted, thin blades were used puzzles archaeologists.

This resource-rich region, between Kenai and Skilak lakes, contains not only the oldest site on the peninsula but many younger sites as well. It was the

LEFT: *These 4,000-year-old artifacts, projectile points, bipoints, scrapers, an adze and knives, from upper Kachemak Bay sites are similar in style and material to tools excavated along the Brooks River on the Alaska Peninsula. Some archaeologists interpret this find as evidence that Alaska Peninsula people hunted land animals in upper Kachemak Bay. (Janet R. Klein)*

FACING PAGE: *In 1993, these Kenaitze Dena'ina dancers helped dedicate the Kenaitze Interpretive Site along the Kenai River near Cooper Landing. This archaeological site in Chugach National Forest holds house and cache pits that were being disturbed by campers and fishermen launching boats. The area was closed to those uses, an interpretive trail was built, and the Kenaitze Indian Tribe took over the site's management in agreement with the U.S. Forest Service. The tribe also provides an interpreter at the site, which is marked by a sign at mile 54 of the Sterling Highway. (David Rhode)*

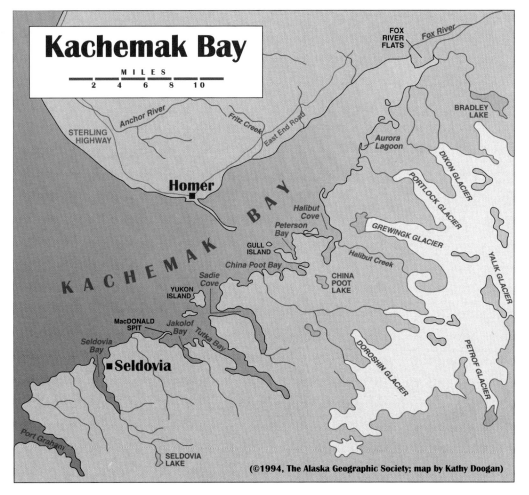

Kachemak Bay

MILES
2 4 6 8 10

STERLING
HIGHWAY

Anchor River

Fritz Creek

East End Road

FOX RIVER FLATS

Fox River

BRADLEY LAKE

Aurora Lagoon

Homer

DIXON GLACIER

PORTLOCK GLACIER

Halibut Cove

Peterson Bay

GREWINGK GLACIER

GULL ISLAND

Halibut Creek

YALIK GLACIER

China Poot Bay

Sadie Cove

CHINA POOT LAKE

KACHEMAK BAY

YUKON ISLAND

MacDONALD SPIT

Jakolof Bay

Tutka Bay

DOROSHIN GLACIER

PETROF GLACIER

Seldovia Bay

■ Seldovia

Port Graham

SELDOVIA LAKE

(©1994, The Alaska Geographic Society; map by Kathy Doogan)

traditional hunting and fishing territory of the Kenaitze Dena'ina Indians. Unique among Athabaskans, the Dena'ina moved from dry-land interior Alaska to the Cook Inlet coast about 1,000 years ago, and adopted many marine-related hunting, fishing and survival techniques from their Eskimo predecessors.

Fishing the waters of the Kenai and Russian rivers was the Dena'ina's main economy. Hundreds of cache pits lining the riverbanks attest to the importance of fish. Other depressions may identify former sites of summer dwellings, small tentlike, pole structures covered with bark and skins. Large rectangular depressions, often with smaller, attached rooms, indicate more substantial winter homes. Abundant fire-cracked rock points to the use of bath houses.

The Dena'ina call the region *Sqilantnu*, and in 1880 it was home to at least 44 Dena'ina according to U.S. Census taker Ivan Petroff. Several years later, most of the Dena'ina had moved downriver, to the mouth of the Kenai. But in recognition of its outstanding concentration of prehistoric and historic sites, the Sqilantnu Archaeological District was created by the state's Office of History and Archaeology. Encompassing about 3,240 acres of river valley and lower mountainsides, Sqilantnu stretches for about four miles between Kenai and Skilak lakes.

The Dena'ina returned to Sqilantnu in 1993 and opened *Hchan'lyut*, a summer interpretive center on the banks of the Kenai. To help protect the archaeological sites, tribal members tell visitors about the rich prehistory of the region, about why the sites are important and how to avoid damaging them.

The prehistory of the Kenai Peninsula is rich and complex. Many cultures lived here, especially along the salmon-rich rivers of the upper peninsula and the productive marine coast of the lower peninsula. Often, different cultures were attracted to the same locality and lived atop the remains of former inhabitants. Shell middens, or ancient refuse piles, cache pits, house depressions, rock paintings, rock shelters, piles of fire-cracked rocks and occasional artifacts eroding from sites confirm the widespread distribution of prehistoric people on the peninsula.

Some prehistoric sites are small, just an overhanging rock that provided temporary shelter. A fire hearth, a few bones from a meal and an occasional artifact reveal its use by humans. Others are considerably larger and contain dozens of house or cache pit depressions. The confluence of the Moose and Kenai rivers, near present-day Sterling, was the site of a sizeable settlement about 1000 B.C. Today's visitors to the Izaak Walton State Recreation Site in Sterling camp, fish and boat in the same productive region as people did thousands of years ago.

Small sites are scattered along bluff tops and near stream mouths from the Kasilof River southward to Kachemak Bay where another major concentration of prehistoric people lived. Kachemak Bay, a cornucopia-shaped embayment, slices 39 miles into the Kenai Peninsula, separating the glacially sculpted Kenai Mountains from the Kenai Lowlands. Prehistoric people lived primarily on the islands and headlands of the convoluted coast from Kachemak Bay to Resurrection Bay.

Five distinct cultures have been identified from archaeological sites in Kachemak Bay. These skilled seafarers who settled lower Cook Inlet came from Prince William Sound, the Kodiak archipelago and the Alaska Peninsula. In bidarkas or kayaks they boated great distances to hunt, to gather food and to trade information and valuables such as jasper, jet and ivory. Occasionally, they exchanged slaves, waged war and took hostages.

Among the oldest site on the southern peninsula is a small encampment in upper Kachemak Bay. Almost 5,000 years ago, Ocean Bay people, from Kodiak or the Alaska Peninsula, journeyed to the bay and camped alongside Aurora Lagoon. Whole and broken tools, especially chert flakes and slate lance blades, reveal their presence. The long slate blades, with distinctive notched edges, suggest that these were marine

Gladys and Fred Elvsaas, of Seldovia, marvel at an artifact found by Susan Springer, left, during the first archaeological excavation in Seldovia in May 1993. A radiocarbon date indicates that the small shell midden site was occupied about 1450 A.D. (Janet R. Klein)

mammal hunters, possibly summer visitors harvesting seals, porpoises, sea lions and small whales. A catastrophic volcanic eruption spewed tons of ash and pumice over Kachemak Bay about 3,000 years ago. When archaeologists excavated the Ocean Bay encampment in 1992, a 3-inch-thick layer of grayish ash sealed the site.

Frederica de Laguna, who pioneered archaeological field work on the Kenai Peninsula during the early 1930s, defined and described the Kachemak tradition, which followed the Ocean Bay culture and is the best known and longest lived culture on the peninsula.

Kachemak tradition people occupied the Kenai Peninsula for about 2,500 years. The Riverine

Kachemak people adapted to life along upper peninsula rivers; simultaneously, their southern relatives, the Marine Kachemak people, adapted to life along the coastal fringes of the lower peninsula.

Great piles of discarded shells and bones, and occasional artifacts and human remains, characterize large Marine Kachemak sites. Analysis of midden materials reveals that these people enjoyed a great variety of foods, including seal and porpoise, whales,

LEFT: *Many groups of early people moved through the Kenai Peninsula. The different cultures often used the same places, living atop remains of former inhabitants. This archaeological excavation in Halibut Cove revealed a Dena'ina Indian house that had been built over an older Eskimo site. (David Rhode)*

BELOW: *Chert outcroppings reveal early forces that helped shape the peninsula. Intense heat and pressure fractured, folded and uplifted radiolarian chert beds that formed much of the southern end of the Kenai Mountain range. Radiolarian are tiny, single-celled marine animals. Chert is a flintlike rock containing quartz and silica. (Arne Bakke)*

The land between Kenai and Skilak lakes holds many archaeological sites, attesting to plentiful resources found there by early people. The peninsula's oldest known prehistoric site, about 8,000 years old, is in this area near Cooper Landing. An excavation of ancient house pits in Cooper Landing, shown here, took place during summer 1984, because the site was in the path of a proposed highway realignment. Mona Painter, a local historian who was volunteering on this dig, bends over a screen to sift dirt away from artifacts. The highway did not go through here, and proposed routes were still being vigorously debated in 1994. (Helen Rhode)

seabirds, clams, mussels, sea urchins, cod and halibut, and land animals, such as marmot, caribou and bear. Frederica de Laguna dug through a 15-foot-thick shell midden at a large Marine Kachemak site on Yukon Island, near the entrance to inner Kachemak Bay.

The Marine Kachemak people enjoyed a relatively bountiful existence. Although disease, warfare, starvation and unusual mortuary practices, such as dismemberment, burial of body parts within the houses and inserting of artificial eyes in the skeleton, are evident, they developed a complex culture that included stone and bone tools and elaborately decorated art pieces. Selected traits common in Marine Kachemak sites include grooved stones, notched stones becoming smaller as time passed, slate blades and ulus, toggle harpoon heads and barbed bone darts. Fine bone awls and delicately eyed needles, baked shale beads and large, intricately decorated stone lamps with raised knobs or animal or human figures in the bowl, display their artistic skills.

Pictographs, images on rock, were painted with red ochre. Geometric designs, tiny inch-high human figures, kayaks, whales, seals and unidentified anthropomorphs, humanlike forms, are found at four sites in Kachemak Bay. Some archaeologists attribute them to the Marine Kachemak people.

These people disappeared from the archaeological record around 500 to 900 A.D. Archaeologists are puzzled as to why a seemingly successful culture would disappear from the Kenai Peninsula after 2,500 years.

Providing a link to the past and a continuum with the future are the contemporary Native people of the Kenai Peninsula. Like their predecessors, many members of the Kenaitze Dena'ina tribe live in the Kenai-Soldotna area. When Russian fur trappers entered peninsula waters in the late 1700s, Dena'ina were occupying the region from Seldovia to the Matanuska Valley east of Anchorage.

Native residents of Port Graham, Nanwalek (formerly English Bay) and Seldovia, villages near the peninsula's tip, trace their heritage to Prince William Sound, the Gulf of Alaska, Kodiak, the Aleutian Islands and the Alaska Peninsula, and their population on the Kenai Peninsula was fairly stable until influenza, smallpox and measles, introduced by Caucasians, decimated their numbers in the epidemics of the 1830s, 1884 and 1918.

Today, many Natives are experiencing a resurgence of interest in their heritage. Languages are being relearned and recorded, ancient crafts revitalized, traditions re-established. Port Graham, Nanwalek

TOP LEFT: *The peninsula's early people hunted, fished and gathered a variety of foods from land and sea. These included caribou, bear, seals, whales, cod, halibut, ducks, geese, clams, mussels and snails. Hairy tritons, a type of sea snail, hatch from eggs like these laid on rocks in the intertidal zone. (Janet R. Klein)*

LEFT: *Sandhill cranes, here seen near Homer, are among nearly two dozen species of migrating waterfowl that seasonally feed, nest and stage on the Kenai Peninsula. The arrival of birds each spring meant fresh meat and eggs to early people, hungry from dwindling winter food stocks. (Chlaus Lotscher)*

This Landsat image gives an overall view of the Kenai Peninsula. As with all false-color images, reddish-brown indicates areas of vegetation; white represents areas of snow and ice; the dark blue is Cook Inlet and the Gulf of Alaska; and the turquoise blue in the middle of the reddish-brown area is Tustumena Lake. (Courtesy of Janet R. Klein)

and Kenai have dance groups that are rediscovering the ancient art of storytelling through music and movement.

The Native American Graves Protection and Repatriation Act of 1990 calls for the return of human remains and burial goods to groups requesting them. In September 1993, the remains of more than 82 Chugach Alutiiq people, excavated about 60 years earlier, were reinterred on Yukon Island in Kachemak Bay.

Current knowledge of prehistoric people and the environment of the Kenai Peninsula has been defined and refined primarily through archaeological excavation. In addition to Frederica de Laguna's pioneering archaeological research, Cornelius Osgood undertook ethnographic research on the peninsula in the early 1930s. Almost 40 years elapsed before a resurgence of interest attracted Alan Boraas, of Soldotna, and Douglas Reger, Charles Holmes, Karen and William Workman and Peter Zollars, of Anchorage, and numerous others to the peninsula.

Many questions, however, remain unanswered. Who were the first people to inhabit the peninsula? When did they arrive and, from where? Why did successful cultures, such as the Kachemak tradition, disappear from the archaeological record? What environmental or physiological changes, if any, caused their exodus or their decline?

The prehistoric resources of the Kenai Peninsula are irreplaceable and few in number. Contemporary people, who occupy the same river and coastal lands as prehistoric people, often damage or destroy sites. Natural erosion takes a daily toll on coastal sites. Knowledge and understanding of the human history of the Kenai Peninsula and of how people relate to the land depends upon responsible stewardship of our Native heritage.

Stretching from the southwestern tip northward along the western edge of the Kenai Peninsula are five communities whose heritage is Russian: Nanwalek, Port Graham, Seldovia, Kenai and Ninilchik. A Russian Orthodox church stands as a spiritual and cultural center of each community.

Under the Czar

Nanwalek

By Janet R. Klein

Nanwalek, formerly English Bay, is the oldest historic settlement on mainland Alaska. Although Native people used the area before the Russians came, the history of Nanwalek begins in 1785-86 when Alexandrovsk Redoubt (Fort Alexander) was established by Grigorii Shelikov, who was expanding his quest for new sea otter hunting grounds. The fort site, centered on the sand spit which separates English Bay Lagoon from Cook Inlet, was covered when an airport runway was constructed atop it in the 1950s.

Missionaries and schoolteachers, espousing the Russian Orthodox religion, followed the trading companies and, today, most residents attend the Saints Sergius and Herman of Valaam Church. The

LEFT: *Many people like to dig for razor clams on the western peninsula's sandy beaches between Kasilof and Anchor Point. Sport fishing licenses are required. These men are digging at Clam Gulch, where thousands of clams are dug each year. (Chlaus Lotscher)*

FACING PAGE: *The Russian Orthodox chapel and cemetery of the Holy Transfiguration of Our Lord crowns a bluff overlooking Ninilchik. The building is the centerpiece of one of the most popular photos taken during a Kenai summer, when pink fireweed surrounds the picturesque structure. (Alaskana Photo-Art)*

The village of Nanwalek faces Cook Inlet on the southern peninsula. Russian traders built a fort at this site in 1785, making it the oldest historic settlement on mainland Alaska. Nanwalek, formerly English Bay, is reached by boat or airplane. (David Roseneau)

original church, built in 1890 and listed on the National Register of Historic Places, is no longer used. A new one sits alongside it, on a hillside overlooking Cook Inlet.

The Alaska Commercial Co. took over the Fort Alexander trading post not long after the United States purchased Alaska in 1867. Forty-two years later, when the U.S. Geological Survey mapped the Kenai Peninsula, the name English Bay was accidentally applied to Fort Alexander. The new name stuck until 1991 when Nanwalek was adopted. A Pacific Eskimo word, Nanwalek means "place with a lagoon" and refers to the rich intertidal lagoon adjacent to the village.

As trading declined and a cash economy developed, Nanwalek residents were forced to leave home. Throughout the years, they've engaged in commercial fishing and worked in fish processing plants, primarily in nearby Port Graham. Although employment opportunities remain limited, borough, state and Native corporation jobs offer work in town. The village council owns a store that employs several people and logging provides temporary jobs.

Nanwalek's 180 residents have chosen to remain rather isolated. Without a harbor or a dock few Outsiders visit, and residents beach their boats in winter, increasing community isolation. Several Homer-based airlines serve Nanwalek year-round, otherwise skiffs or the corporation barge haul goods and people. All-terrain vehicles take the place of cars. Because it has chosen to remain inaccessible, Nanwalek retains much of its original flavor.

Subsistence fishing, hunting and gathering remain important to the well-being of residents. In 1987, the average household harvest of natural resources was 1,139 pounds of fish, seal, sea lion, porcupine, bear, birds, intertidal foods such as clams and bidarkies or chitons, and a variety of edible plants and berries. When oil from the *Exxon Valdez* spill in Prince William Sound fouled the shoreline, rendering seafoods inedible, Native residents from other coastal communities shipped fresh foods to Nanwalek. Five years after the spill, select beaches remain closed to the taking of subsistence foods.

A rudimentary road was recently extended south eight miles to Koyuktolik (Dogfish) Bay, providing improved access to moose, mountain goat and waterfowl habitat, berry patches, additional fishing and a change of scenery. Put simply, the road offers a chance to get out of town. And, villagers can travel to Port Graham via water or a four-mile trail through the woods.

The residents control much of their destiny. A handful of Nanwalek women, who have obtained education degrees in other states, are returning to teach. A local Village Public Safety Officer polices Nanwalek, a difficult task when patrolling relatives. As in the past, elders or lay people conduct regular services in the Russian Orthodox chapel and an itinerant priest routinely visits Nanwalek, Port Graham and Seldovia.

Residents of Nanwalek and Port Graham are members of Chugach Alaska Corp., headquartered in Anchorage, yet each community retains its own village council and governs itself.

As to the future, the Village Council identified the following goals: preserve the village character, maintain village control, enhance the quality of life and protect the environment and their subsistence-based culture, strong goals yet certainly obtainable in this community near the tip of the Kenai Peninsula.

A group of sport fishermen show off their day's catch from a halibut charter out of Homer. (Cary Anderson)

Port Graham

By Janet R. Klein

Confusion occasionally arises when discussing Port Graham for the name applies to the waterway and to the Alutiiq village clustered midway along its southern shore. *Paluwik*, the Alutiiq name formerly used for this area means "where the people are sad," a reference to the deliberate consolidation of people from villages in the Gulf of Alaska and Prince William Sound in the late 1890s to begin the present-day community. One explanation for this movement is that Russian Orthodox priests began to consolidate their parishes as they built churches and schools. This occurred even after the United States purchased Alaska in 1867.

Capt. Nathaniel Portlock, who sailed with Capt. James Cook in 1778, returned to the region in 1786. He noticed numerous abandoned huts, presumably the former homes of Native residents who used the area long before the present community originated. Portlock also discovered coal outcroppings in a bight near the mouth of a 7-mile-long embayment. He named the bight, Coal Bay, and the waterway, Grahams Harbor. Today, they are called Coal Cove and Port Graham.

About 70 years later, the Russian American Co., seeking new sources of income, opened the first coal mine on North America's Pacific coast near the mouth of Port Graham bay. Enoch Furuhjelm, a Finnish entrepreneur, headed the enterprise from about 1857 to 1861. Although coal was shipped to the West Coast, commercial markets never developed. Metal leg shackles found in the area indicate that forced labor was used, in part, to mine the seaside seams.

Port Graham village has a progressive, forward-looking feeling. The community supports two grocery stores, a small cafe, a library, an experimental research fish hatchery and a community/activity center. The center houses the post office, and offices for the Village Public Safety Officer and an alcohol program and counselor.

Many comfortable, frame houses line the airport or waterfront and were constructed with HUD funds. All have electricity and running water. Most residents heat with spruce cut nearby; a few own cars, most own boats and often run their skiffs to Homer. Several Homer barge companies provide regular service to the

The Alutiiq village of Port Graham faces a bay off Cook Inlet. Its nearest neighbor is Nanwalek, four miles to the west. The village is reached by boat or commuter flights out of Homer. The cannery complex in the foreground belongs to the Port Graham Corp. (Steve McCutcheon)

community along the southern shore of Port Graham.

Daily commuter flights connect Port Graham with Homer, about 15 to 20 minutes away. Residents of Port Graham and Nanwalek are discussing construction of one airport located between their villages; the Nanwalek runway, exposed directly to Cook Inlet, washes out occasionally.

As at Nanwalek, traditional foods are gathered in season. Although select beaches remain closed due to oil pollution from the *Exxon Valdez* spill, the 170 residents still gather edible plants and herbs, seaweed and chitons and hunt a variety of terrestrial animals.

Donna Fenske, a public health nurse living in Homer, has visited Port Graham and Nanwalek regularly since 1979. The gentleness of the people has won her heart and she encourages others to become acquainted with them. Fedora's Bed and Breakfast, at the east end of Port Graham, is open year-round. Visitors can fish from the beach, pick berries, hike the few trails or simply relax in the laid-back atmosphere.

Port Graham has a mixed subsistence-cash economy. Employment is usually seasonal and often sporadic, such as in logging camps on the outer peninsula coast. In 1984, the Port Graham Corp. purchased a fish processing plant, currently the community's major employer. Various state, federal and borough positions, such as health aides, educators and the postmaster, provide additional employment as do the village corporation and village council.

The local tribal council and Chugachmiut, a health and social service agency, have initiated programs for children that focus on their Native/Russian heritage. According to Elenore McMullen, village chief, a sobriety movement has strengthened the family network, resulting in increasing parental involvement with school and youth activities.

The first female chief of the village, Elenore follows Walter Meganack Sr., who served 31 years before retiring. She actively encourages community unity

Jon Osgood of Tutka Bay Lodge carefully walks on logs rafted next to a Korean freighter in Kasitsna Bay. Native groups have logged portions of their land and sold the timber to businesses in the Orient. Logging on the southern peninsula has been controversial for years. Groups owning land with marketable trees say that selling the timber is the only way they can earn revenue from their land. Others maintain that forested mountainsides are more valuable than slopes marked by clearcuts. One of the most vigorously contested environmental debates on the southern peninsula in recent years involved proposed logging of Seldovia Native Association lands on the south side of Kachemak Bay. This long-standing issue was finally resolved in the early 1990s when the state agreed to buy the land and timber contracts. (Penny Rennick)

and the revitalization of traditional crafts and activities. Basketmaking, beading, wood carving and skin sewing are once again being taught along with languages and dancing. Village residents are dedicated to improving their economy while retaining and enhancing their cultural heritage.

Nikolaevsk, Island of the Faith

By Bob Moore

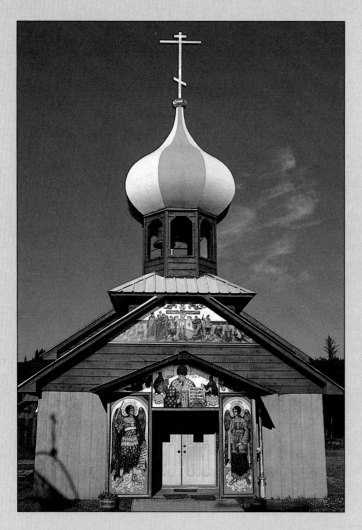

Images of Archangels Gabriel and Michael guard the entrance to the church at Nikolaevsk. St. Nikolai looks down from above the door, while higher up is a depiction of the Crucifixion. (Chlaus Lotscher)

Editor's note: *A resident of Homer and now retired, Bob Moore was for years the principal of the Nikolaevsk school.*

More than one homesteader thought it and some matter-of-factly stated, "They will never make it." After the devastating tent fire that took the life of one child and left a woman scarred for life that winter, others emphatically declared, "They will be gone before snow falls again."

But they didn't go and some of us have had the privilege to know and work with them through 25 winters. Little did we know then of the determination, tenacity or work ethic of these newcomers to the Kenai Peninsula. But we've come to recognize those traits and many others that distinguish the Old Believers of Nikolaevsk. These Russian immigrants, the Old Believers, first showed up on the peninsula in 1967. Five bearded representatives of the 300-year-old religious group were looking for land where an "island of the faith" could be established. They found that land east of Anchor Point where the foothills join the spruce forests leading back to Cook Inlet. There they purchased one square mile of land from the state.

The Nikolaevsk Old Believers are a remnant of a group that once numbered in the millions. Millions were lost throughout the years from persecution by the Orthodox Church, the government and eventually Stalin's purge of the masses. Survivors almost completely circled the globe seeking religious freedom before settling here.

The first families came in fall 1968 and lived in tents on land nearby while trees were cleared and the first buildings were built. It was during this time the fire occurred that caused the first death in the new community. Within a few weeks, however, a new baby girl born in Nikolaevsk brought renewed optimism.

Nikolaevsk became a reality on Dec. 19, 1968, and was named after St. Nikolai, Orthodoxy's patron saint of that date. New residents arrived soon from Oregon and added their energy to developing the site. A church was built before most of the homes were completed. Roads were laid out and a water supply was developed and lines installed. Work was like worship and the synergy from many hands with a common purpose accomplished miraculous results.

A school was established in March 1970 among ripsawn cabins, berms and new garden plots. Twenty-one children in grades one to eight took time out from woodcutting, cow tending and baby-sitting to attend the one-room trailer school. It only held 14 student desks so creative teaching and continuous adjustments were necessary.

New residents, new homes, new children and a renewed interest in education resulted in 43 children being in school by November 1970. A new building was planned, but proved inadequate before it was completed. During the next few years, this resulted in continual catch-up programs with as many as five buildings being used as school classrooms at one time. A new, six-room school was built in 1976 and an addition with six classrooms, a beautiful Russian/English library and a multipurpose room was added in 1981.

Residents walked the mile and one-half

from Nikolaevsk to the main road to find rides to work in the canneries, boat shops and construction sites of Homer and the surrounding area. Some worked in Anchorage and as far away as Dutch Harbor.

Children and adults alike seem to have a "work hard when you work, play hard when you play" philosophy. Adults have little free time and children are often involved in sewing, embroidery or woodworking. Gardens need tending, housework must be done and siblings require constant care. Study of holy books is mandatory during fasting periods prior to Christmas and Easter.

More than 50 homes were in Nikolaevsk in the early 1980s. At about that time, differences of opinion in religious issues resulted in several families moving and establishing four new communities near the head of Kachemak Bay. Kachemak Selo was the first and currently is home to about 200 residents. Voznesenka has a similar number, while Razdolna has about 15 families. Dolina once was home to about 60 people, but is so remote and inaccessible that only about three families live there now. A group has established a small community on Raspberry Island near Kodiak, while another group is near Willow, north of Anchorage in the Susitna Valley.

The Old Believers have more than 50 boats in their fishing fleet. They continue to work in area businesses and have established some businesses of their own. They have some exceptional students in their schools and attending college. Their lives revolve around their religious beliefs as they interact with the dominant culture. They maintain their uniqueness, while making the peninsula a stronger, more humane and more tolerant place to live, work and play.

ABOVE: *During the wedding of Daniel and Luba Dorvall, the wedding party proceeds from the Church of St. Nikolai to the bride's home. Before the couple reach the home, the bride's parents offer bread and salt to the groom to welcome their new son-in-law into the family. (Bob Moore)*

LEFT: *Agafia Molidik teaches Tonia Fefelov (right) and another student at the school at Nikolaevsk. (Bob Moore)*

Seldovia

By Janet R. Klein

The historic waterfront community of Seldovia lines Seldovia Bay near the southern entrance to Kachemak Bay. Accessible only by air or water, it has retained much of its character and historic flavor.

Seldovia is served year-round by commuter airlines with daily 12-minute flights from Homer and, in summer, by private boats, charter boats and the Alaska Marine Highway System. Traditionally, the state ferry *Tustumena* runs twice a week in summer and links Seldovians with Kodiak and points farther south and west. In 1993, four charter boats cruised daily between Homer and Seldovia from Memorial to Labor Day. Most dock for two hours, just enough time to see the highlights and vow to return. The seaside community is about an hour boat trip southwest of Homer.

Seldovia's heritage is Native and Russian. According to Fred Elvsaas, president of the Seldovia Village Tribe, Seldovia Bay was a meeting and trading place for Koniags from Kodiak, Chugach Alutiiq from Prince William Sound and the Dena'ina of Cook Inlet long before Russians came to Alaska.

Russian influence is visible in the St. Nicholas Russian Orthodox Church, which overlooks the entrance to 5-mile-long Seldovia Bay. This National Historic Landmark was built in 1891. Long after the purchase of Alaska in 1867, itinerant Russian priests conducted services and missionaries taught school in the former Native village. The name, "Z(aliv) Seldevoy," or herring bay, appeared on 1852 maps compiled by Capt. Mikhail Tebenkov, a cartographer with the Imperial Russian Navy. Whether an actual Russian-based community existed at that time, remains unknown. Throughout much of the 1800s Russian and American trading posts operated in Seldovia, where sea otter pelts were an important commodity.

All the amenities of a small town are here: cafes and restaurants, churches, two hotels, bed and breakfasts, a library, a pharmacy, a medical clinic and, down the road, a wilderness lodge. The Seldovia Native Association, headquartered here, has a small museum, with prehistoric and historic artifacts, and a tribal store.

LEFT: *Canoe boxing in the small boat harbor is a highlight of Independence Day celebrations at Seldovia. (Penny Rennick)*

FACING PAGE: *Mount Iliamna, 10,016 feet, looms across Cook Inlet in the Alaska-Aleutian Range in this view from Seldovia. Residents from Anchor Point north to Ninilchik have talked about building a volcano observatory along this stretch of the Sterling Highway that follows the bluff overlooking the inlet. (Gail Richards)*

Historically, Seldovia was the social, economic, cultural and spiritual center for lower Cook Inlet during the first half of this century. The well-protected, deep-water bay was the port of entry for gold and coal miners, fur trappers and traders, explorers, tourists and hunters traveling to the Kenai Peninsula.

Pride of old Seldovia was the boardwalk built in 1930-31 with local money and muscle. The half-mile-long walkway connected canneries, salteries and businesses, and smaller catwalks led to hillside homes. Eventually the boardwalk was widened to accommodate cars.

Fishing and fish processing have been the mainstay of Seldovia since the trading posts disappeared. A herring boom, from 1911 to 1928, brought hundreds of seasonal workers to town. Commercial salmon fishing began about the same time and, through the years, Seldovians fished the once-productive waters of Kachemak Bay for salmon; king, Dungeness and Tanner crab; and five species of shrimp. The prosperous community supported at least four canneries and a cold storage plant before 1964.

The March 27, 1964, earthquake changed Seldovia. As elsewhere on the southern peninsula, the land subsided. When tides flooded boardwalk canneries and processing plants, a historic era ended. Although controversial, urban renewal removed the businesses

TOP LEFT: *This 1950 view north along the Seldovia waterfront shows the canneries and a portion of the boardwalk that were the town's signature. Seldovia was the main commercial center on Kachemak Bay for many years. (William Wakeland)*

LEFT: *Living by the sea means coping with its extremes. In Seldovia, waterfront homes perch on tall pilings to stay clear of high tides rising 23 feet or more. These homes face Seldovia Slough on the edge of town. (Janet R. Klein)*

and all but a short remnant of the boardwalk. With the loss of the canneries, Seldovia's prominence in Kachemak Bay dwindled. The 1980 population of 479 dropped to 316 in 1990 and, when the John Cabot cannery closed in the early 1990s, another 40 to 60 people moved away.

Seldovians face tough decisions about their future. In 1994, a movement was underway to dissolve the city government. With less than 300 residents, some feel it is a luxury they can no longer afford. An Economic Development and Tourism Study, in 1993, listed fish processing, tourism, arts and crafts and wilderness education as potential economic opportunities, yet only a few of those would offer strong, long-term benefits to city coffers. The Native association logs on the end of the peninsula, rents property and plans to quarry large rocks in Seldovia Bay for construction projects elsewhere.

Tourism offers a bright light for those who endorse it. More than 16,000 people visited in 1992, mostly for day trips. Visitors, walking around the small community, can view locally produced arts and crafts at Synergy Art Works, amble along the remnant boardwalk, relax in several pocket parks, climb a short, steep hill to view the Russian Orthodox church, and learn about the town's colorful history from many handsome signs erected in 1993.

The highlight of Seldovia's summer is the Fourth of July. An old-fashioned parade, community picnic and a variety of games, such as canoe boxing, the log roll and climbing the greased pole to snatch the money atop it, entertain viewers and participants. Other summer activities include fishing, digging butter clams, kayaking, hiking and berry-picking. Twenty-eight inches of rain a year stimulate dense patches of blueberries, currants and the local favorite, salmonberries.

Peaks of the Kenai Mountains, some 3,000 feet high, provide a stunning background and playground for

The seaside town of Seldovia, population about 300, entices visitors with its scenery, rich history and charming ambiance. (Jon R. Nickles)

visitors who overnight. Open tundra beckons hikers, berry-pickers, skiers and snowmobilers to venture above the spruce-covered slopes where stunning views of Cape Douglas and mounts Augustine, Iliamna and Redoubt reward those who persevere.

The 13-mile-long Jakolof Bay Road, heading east from Seldovia, ends a few miles beyond an old logging camp. A hiking and biking trail climbs to the abandoned chromium mines at Red Mountain or passes through the mountains to Windy Bay on the Gulf of Alaska.

Seldovians are resilient folks. Their roots and pride extend deep into the history of the Kenai Peninsula. Those who can weather economically unstable times will keep the community alive and viable for it has too much to offer for it to be otherwise.

Kenai

By Janet R. Klein

Kenai, largest city on the peninsula, calls itself the "Village with a past, City with a future." Kenai's roots began in a land already the home of the Kenaitze Dena'ina, from whom the town and river took their name. The second peninsula's oldest Russian community, Kenai originated in 1791 as an outpost.

The Kenai Bicentennial Visitors and Cultural Center, built in 1991 for the town's 200th year celebration, has wildlife exhibits, interpretive displays and films as well as visitor information. The center is open daily June through August. (Ron Levy)

Commanded by Gregory Konovalov, Fort St. Nicholas (Nikolaevsk Redoubt), provided access to the Kenai Mountains for Russian fur traders and trappers expanding their territory. When British explorer

The St. Nicholas Russian Orthodox Chapel was erected in downtown Kenai in 1906 to commemorate the town's first resident priest, Igumen Nicholai. He is buried underneath the chapen with two other church members. (Harry M. Walker)

Capt. George Vancouver visited in 1794, he noted that about 40 Russians occupied the outpost. As elsewhere, the Russian Orthodox religion took hold, and the oldest buildings in Kenai are Orthodox-related: the rectory, a photogenic log structure built about 1886; the present Holy Assumption of the Virgin Mary Orthodox Church, built in 1895; and the log chapel nearby, built about 1906.

Two years after the purchase of Alaska from Russia, the Americans took over Fort St. Nicholas, calling it Fort Kenay. Log walls and two blockhouses protected a barracks, church and priest's residences. The Americans added a guardhouse, quartermaster's offices, commissary, kitchen, blacksmith shop and stables, and a hospital. A replica of the log fort, erected in 1967 during the Alaska Centennial, and the nearby Russian Orthodox rectory, chapel and church constitute Old Kenai or Old Town.

Kenai is 161 scenic road miles southwest of Anchorage or a 30-minute commuter flight over Turnagain Arm and across the muskeg and lakes of the northern peninsula. Daily flights link Kenai with Kodiak, Anchorage and Homer.

All modern services are available in Kenai, including fast-food chain stores, international cuisine, shopping malls and a Kmart. A host of retail, commercial and professional services available in the 28.5 square miles of this first class city serve peninsula residents.

Kenai actively supports heavy industry, especially petroleum-based industries. Black gold provides economic stability for many of the residents. Onshore, Atlantic Richfield struck oil in the Swanson River fields in 1957, igniting the boom. Offshore, Shell Oil

discovered huge oil and gas fields under the murky waters of Cook Inlet. By 1970, bustling industry had swept aside the small, sleepy community.

The push to find new oil fields on the Kenai and offshore in Cook Inlet continues. In 1993, Unocal announced continued efforts to enhance recovery from their offshore fields, and Arco Alaska Inc. toasted their Sunfish prospect, a field in Cook Inlet whose boundaries are still being delineated.

Kenai residents play as hard as they work. The city is home to baseball's Peninsula Oilers, a semi-professional team in the Alaska League. Five Little League fields are crowded all summer. With almost 20 hours of light, days can be stretched to include baseball and fishing.

Outside the city are thousands of square miles of lakes, streams and rivers, offering a wide variety of activities. Sport fishing is number one, with residents and summer visitors. The fish-choked rivers beckon anglers all summer. The Kenai provides salmon fishing for kings, reds, silver and chum. Commercial and setnet fishermen deliver their catch to canneries lining the river's mouth.

Kenai offers unique wildlife watching opportunities. In the past decade highway personnel have prepared pull-offs adjacent to the highway bridge over

TOP LEFT: *The Warren Ames Bridge crosses the Kenai River south of Kenai. A state recreation site with a parking lot and boardwalk near the bridge is a good place to watch caribou and migrating watrerfowl such as Siberian snow geese on the Kenai River Flats. (Ron Levy)*

LEFT: *Kenai, population 6,300, has grown from a Russian trading post established more than 200 years ago into the largest city on the peninsula. This photo shows the main road through town and part of the core commercial area. The main road continues to the left to the industrial area at Nikiski. (Ron Levy)*

the Kenai flats near the river's mouth. Each April viewers can spot hundreds of snow geese, migrating to nesting grounds on Russia's Wrangel Island from wintering areas along the Pacific coast. Feeding with the snow geese are smaller numbers of Canada geese, white-fronted geese, mallards and northern pintails. Sandhill cranes pluck grubs and larvae from the flats and bald eagles perch on the tall spruce that fringe the marshlands. Occasionally, the local herd of caribou grazes on the flats. Beluga whales pursue fish into the lower stretches of the Kenai River and can be observed from the 100-foot-high bluff near the river's mouth.

Kenai celebrated its bicentennial in 1991 by constructing the Kenai Bicentennial Visitors and

Many Kenai residents work in the petroleum industry. The Tesoro Alaska refinery at Nikiski, north of Kenai, was built in 1969 and in 1994 employed 143 permanent workers. Most of the plant's refined product is sold or distributed in Alaska; the residuals, the heavy No. 6 oil that settles to the bottom of the tanks, is exported to the Lower 48 and Asia. When operating at maximum capacity, the refinery produces 72,000 barrels per day. (Marlon Collins, courtesy of Tesoro Alaska)

Cultural Center. The cultural and natural history exhibits provide an in-depth look at the region's resources. The future looks bright for Kenai, honored as an All-American City in 1992.

Kenai's Chamber of Commerce operates out of this log cabin across the parking lot from the modern visitor's center. The cabin used to belong to "Moosemeat John" Hedburg, a woodsman who shared moose meat with his neighbors. He disappeared in the late 1940s during a trip on Cook Inlet in his dory. His cabin was later moved into town to this location. (Jim Lavrakas)

Ninilchik

By Janet R. Klein

About halfway between the Kenai-Soldotna area and Homer lies the business district of Ninilchik. The historic community originated on the outwash plain at the mouth of the Ninilchik River, just feet above sea level. Retired Russian American Co. employees, often with Native wives and children, founded Ninilchik about 1835.

Agriculture, fishing, hunting, trapping and gold mining sustained the early residents as did the Russian Orthodox religion. Dominating the hilltop above the old village is the Holy Transfiguration of Our Lord

Chapel and cemetery. Built at the turn of the century and listed on the National Register of Historic Places, the building is still used by many of Ninilchik's 845 residents, and is particularly captivating in late summer when fireweed brightens the hillsides below and 10,016-foot Mount Iliamna looms directly across Cook Inlet. Signs and a walking tour brochure of Ninilchik guide visitors to several log cabins, with dove-tailed corners, and other points of historic interest.

In this century, fur farming, commercial fishing and, more recently, tourism, have supported community growth. The commercial fishing fleet offloads its catch at high tide. A post office, freshwater and saltwater fishing charters, grocery stores, gas stations, several bed and breakfasts and many private and public campgrounds attract a steady stream of summer visitors. Logging on acreage east of town was booming in late 1993. Round logs are trucked from Ninilchik to Homer, where they are stockpiled, chipped and shipped overseas.

The more modern village of Ninilchik, atop a 200-foot-high bluff, straddles the Sterling Highway and contains all the basic facilities and services, especially fishing-related services such as custom taxidermy, and storage and shipping facilities for freshly caught fish. Most summer action in Ninilchik occurs at the mouth of Deep Creek, a mile south of the Ninilchik River.

Ninilchik State Recreation Area and Deep Creek State Recreation Area, with 165 and 300 campsites respectively, are managed by Alaska State Parks. Other state and private campgrounds absorb the overflow from Deep Creek when the salmon are running. Small boats can be launched directly into the creek for access to saltwater fishing for kings, silvers and halibut. The peninsula's unofficial trophy halibut, almost 95 inches long and 460 pounds, was caught by Ninilchik resident, Kathleen McCann, in 1987.

The beaches below the bluffs attract razor clam

diggers and beachcombers. Some come to collect chunks of coal weathered out of seams exposed along this part of the Kenai coast. Birdwatchers are treated to a range of avian species from the bald eagles, glaucous-winged and mew gulls that ride the updrafts just above the bluffs to the warblers, sparrows, chickadees and nuthatches that twitter among the willows, alders and spruce. Where the bluffs give way to river valleys, stately sandhill cranes swiftly strike their prey. Seals, sea otters and small whales are sometimes visible offshore.

The "biggest little fair in Alaska," the Kenai Peninsula State Fair, occurs every August at the local fair grounds. For 43 years, peninsula residents have brought their best: livestock, vegetables, fruits, quilts, homesewn clothes, artwork and a host of other crafts, to be judged and admired. A small rodeo, game booths, food stands, square dancing and other activities provide three days of solid fun.

Winter offers snowmobiling, cross-country skiing, school activities, time to catch up on postponed projects and a little time left over to prepare for next year's fishing, tourism and fair.

TOP LEFT: *The historic settlement of Ninilchik, founded in the early 1800s on the Cook Inlet shore, reflects the fishing commerce of early settlers. As the community grew, expansion occurred on the bluffs overlooking the Ninilchik River and Deep Creek. Today's Ninilchik straddles the Sterling Highway. (George Matz)*

ABOVE: *Throngs of anglers converge each summer at Deep Creek State Recreation Area, immediately south of Ninilchik. They fish for king salmon and halibut in salt-water at the mouth of the creek and salmon and trout in fresh water farther upstream. (Al Grillo)*

The Mountain of Gold

L ike fishing line pulled downstream by strong currents, the Sterling Highway intersects the upper peninsula, stretching westward from its origin at Tern Lake, near Cooper Landing, to Cook Inlet about 50 miles away, then trailing southward to end at the tip of the Homer Spit on Kachemak Bay.

The roadside communities of Cooper Landing, Homer and Anchor Point originated, near the turn of the century, as mining camps. Gold was the flashy lure tempting miners.

Cooper Landing

By Janet R. Klein

Harvesting sea otters pelts for sale in the Orient propelled the eastward expansion of Russia, the push of the promyshlenniki, or fur traders, along the Aleutian Chain and, in the late 1700s, into the Bay of Kenai, as the Russians called Cook Inlet. As sea otter numbers dwindled, other sources of income were

LEFT: *Bald eagles perch on rocks of the Homer Spit breakwater, near a feeding area where cannery scraps are regularly offered by a local woman. The commotion of eagles gorging on fish attracts sightseers, but the feeding practice has become controversial. The number of eagles around Kachemak Bay has increased, perhaps because of this ready food supply. Some people are concerned that the growing population of eagles will displace other birds and animals from the bay, either by chasing them away or killing them off. (Chlaus Lotscher)*

FACING PAGE: *The town of Homer sprawls invitingly along the north shore of Kachemak Bay and onto Homer Spit. The original town with about 150 people sprang up at the end of the spit and was named after Homer Pennock. About 12,000 people live today in Homer, out East End Road and in tiny enclaves across the bay. (Rex Melton)*

Flowers bedeck Dave and Eleanor Young's cabin at Cooper Landing. (Helen Rhode)

sought. Peter Doroshin, a mining engineer with the Russian American Co., ascended the Kenai River in 1848 and found gold near present-day Cooper Landing.

Clearwater tributaries of the Kenai flashed enough color, almost 40 years later, to entice Joseph Cooper from his coal claim on Kachemak Bay. Reportedly, he found gold on an unnamed creek in 1884 yet filed no claim and left for more promising fields. Later, upon returning, he mined the river bars. He died in 1899 but left his name on the landing near his trading post. Other miners, en route overland to Hope or Sunrise, visited Cooper Landing, though never enough gold was discovered to warrant a permanent settlement.

Big game hunting was popular at the turn of the century. Area guides, living near Cooper Landing, sought mountain goat, Dall sheep, bear and, especially, trophy moose for their clients. Wolves, caribou, trophy fish and an abundance of other wildlife were available in the Kenai River valley or nearby.

Flashes of color, in the waterways and on the mountainsides, still attract people to Cooper Landing. The color of wealth, today, is that of silver, pink and red salmon, golden birch-leaves, blue berries, brown moose antlers, rainbow trout and the white Dall sheep, mountain goats and snows found high on the mountains that confine and define this riverside community.

Several gas stations, small cafes, grocery stores, a post office and many fishing, hunting and river-rafting businesses line the forested riverbanks and serve the 300 residents and the tens of thousands of summer visitors.

Cooper Landing is the recreational heart of the Kenai Mountains. When the Seward and Sterling highways are not clogged with vacationers, the community is a two-hour drive south of Anchorage. Public and private campgrounds near Cooper Landing provide more than 400 sites for roadside camping. Many, maintained by the U.S. Forest Service and the U.S. Fish and Wildlife Service, offer trails to the high country. Restless gold miners created the 38-mile Resurrection Pass Trail that begins just west of the Kenai River bridge, climbs to 2,600 feet then descends to sea level near Hope. Berry-picking, lake fishing, photography, mountain biking and cross-country skiing attract a steady flow of adventurers who have reserved the sprinkling of Forest Service cabins along the trail.

Wildlife viewing is popular. Sure-footed Dall sheep drop their lambs on the steep mountain slopes along the north side of Kenai Lake near Cooper Landing and mountain goats feed on Cecil Rhode Mountain, 4,405 feet, on the opposite lakeside. In the narrow, flat Kenai River bottom, moose wade in backwater sloughs to feed on succulent greens.

This is prime fishing country. The Kenai River courses along the Sterling Highway for about 10 miles and, in fishing season, which is all summer, every campground and parking area overflows with people. A privately operated ferry at the Russian River campground hauls passengers to the opposite bank for better access to prime fishing holes. King, red, silver and pink salmon spawn here at different times all summer and rainbow trout, Dolly Varden and whitefish are caught in other lakes and rivers around Cooper Landing.

Where fish congregate, so, too, congregate fish eaters: bald eagles and brown bears. Bears walk the trails, fish the creeks and eat the same berries as people.

A serenity descends upon Cooper Landing in winter. The upper stretches of the Kenai River remain

Pioneer Kenai Peninsula trappers Big and Little Jim inspect their collection of furs at Cooper Landing. (Helen Rhode)

FACING PAGE: *The Nick Lean cabin is one of the earliest structures built at Cooper Landing. (David Rhode)*

ABOVE: *The 1964 Good Friday earthquake shook most of southcentral Alaska. At Cooper Landing residents had to improvise when the quake destroyed the bridge over the Kenai River. (Helen Rhode)*

open and a late run of chum salmon draws resident fishermen and bald eagles. Ice fishing and ice skating on Kenai Lake attract danglers and dancers; snowy trails entice skiers and snowmobilers.

Winter allows time to address local challenges and changes. Freezers are well-stocked with fish and moose meat. Vegetable gardens have been harvested and life resumes a peacefulness unexperienced in summer months. Studies to straighten the Sterling Highway and either widen the roadbed through town or by-pass the community are under consideration. In this small community where tourism is critical to financial stability, any change will have major consequences. In 1994, most residents were leaning toward the by-pass solution. Life here continues its cycle, full speed in summer, relatively slow, quiet and contemplative in winter.

Homer

By Janet R. Klein

Homer, the recreational and commercial center of the southern Kenai Peninsula, sprawls along the benchlands of the north shore of Kachemak Bay. Although about 4,000 residents live within the first-class city, another 8,000 are settled in the spruce forests, along the bluffs and in small enclaves along the mountainous south shore of the bay.

Downtown Homer offers many enticements to stay and play. Popular places to visit include Alaska Wild Berry Products, a locally created business founded by Hazel Heath where jams, jellies and candies are made from hand-picked wild berries; the many art galleries that feature paintings, sculpture, jewelry, clothing, photographs, woodwork and other art and crafts created locally; the Pratt Museum, which focuses on art, culture and natural history; and the Alaska Maritime National Wildlife Refuge visitors' center where displays center on the seabird resources of refuge lands in Alaska. Property on which to construct a new, multimillion dollar center, complete with an exhibit, partly underwater, of living seabirds, has been purchased. As federal funds are forthcoming, planning and construction phases will proceed.

The Homer Spit, 4 and 1/2 miles long, pulls visitors to Kachemak Bay. The spit's thin finger points to the enticing islands and embayments and the snow-capped peaks of the Kenai Mountains

LEFT: *Belva Hamilton shows off her greenhouse tomatoes at Cooper Landing. (Helen Rhode)*

FACING PAGE: *Wreath-maker Claire O'Donnell fashions holiday cheer at her home out East End Road along the northwest shore of Kachemak Bay. (Chlaus Lotscher)*

ABOVE: *Homer, on Kachemak Bay, started as a coal mining community in the late 1800s. This view of town looks west toward Cook Inlet, with Mount Iliamna at upper right. The bluffs behind town rise to a plateau of about 1,200 feet. (Steve McCutcheon)*

RIGHT: *Homesteader Yule Kilcher recently donated development rights to his 620 acres near Homer to Kachemak Heritage Land Trust, one of the first private conservation easement agreement of this type in Alaska. Kilcher left Switzerland during the Nazi buildup prior to World War II, and planned to start a settlement in Alaska for friends who were to follow. But war prevented them from coming, except for Ruth Weber, who arrived from Switzerland in 1941. She and Kilcher married, homesteaded in Homer in 1948, and raised eight children before divorcing. Kilcher served as a delegate to the 1955 Alaska Constitutional Convention and was elected in 1963 from Homer to the state Senate. (David Rhode)*

just minutes away by boat or plane.

The tip of the spit was site of the first community of Homer. In 1896, Homer Pennock, a mining engineer and con man-extraordinaire, maintained a base camp on the spit while he sought gold on Cook Inlet beaches. Lonely, mail-hungry miners named their future post office "Homer." Although gold lured Pennock and his crew to Alaska, they found little on the beaches of Cook Inlet or Kodiak Island. Active mining of coal, however, was occurring along Kachemak Bay and three years later an actual town was built. The coal company town had a large deep-water dock, about 150 employees, 30 or so buildings and a railroad 7 and 3/8 miles long that connected it to the coal mines west of present downtown Homer. The mines produced only subcommercial quality coal and by 1902, Homer was abandoned.

The second town of Homer began in the late 1910s and early 1920s when individuals and families homesteaded on the benchland at the base of the spit. Today, this area is the town's core.

The spit, in summer, serves as the recreational and marine industrial center for the lower peninsula. Where else but at the Fishing Hole can fishermen hook

Anglers encircle the Fishing Hole on Homer Spit. The state stocks this hole with salmon to enhance sport fishing in Kachemak Bay, but the fishery is not self-sustaining since the salmon have no place to spawn when they return. (David Roseneau)

into a salmon most every day of the summer? Thanks to the Alaska Department of Fish and Game which stocks the tiny bight, king, pink and silver salmon return to the hole from mid-May to mid-September. Commercial fishermen bring in their catch from Cook Inlet for processing; dozens of charter boat businesses, eateries and tourist shops, often on pilings above high tides, entice visitors. The small boat harbor offers more than 750 slips to commercial, charter, private and transient boats; and a 30-acre, artificial staging area has become rental space for whatever the city

The Salty Dawg Saloon (at rear) and the General Store reflect the maritime tradition on Homer Spit, site of the original settlement of Homer. (Harry M. Walker)

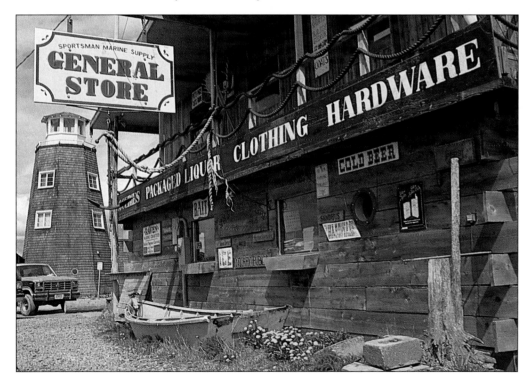

approves. In late 1993, Circle DE Pacific Corp. had a five-year lease to process and store wood chips here. As whole spruce logs are reduced, a yellow mountain of wood chips grows then shrinks rapidly as huge transport ships, anchored at the deep-water dock built in the 1980s, fill their holds and head for Japan.

The spit is also a springboard to action, adventure and activity elsewhere in Cook Inlet. Charter boats travel daily to Gull Island rookery where eight species of seabirds nest; to Halibut Cove and Seldovia, to the Center for Alaskan Coastal Studies at Peterson Bay where guides lead visitors on explorations into the coastal rainforest and, on low tides, into tide pools teeming with life. The 368,000 acres of Kachemak Bay State Park and adjacent State Wilderness Park offer outdoor adventures from berry-picking to glacier skiing. Wildlife viewers board at Homer for excursions to the Barren Islands at the mouth of Cook Inlet to observe seabirds and marine mammals.

Deepsea sport fishing is a major tourist industry. The city sign at the scenic overlook on Bluff Point states that Homer is the halibut capital of the world, the sport-fishing capital, that is. More than 150 charter boats head daily for the halibut grounds from one of the largest man-made small boat harbors in Alaska.

Just two decades ago, a greater wealth of aquatic riches overflowed Kachemak Bay. Commercial fishermen harvested five species of salmon, five of shrimp, three of crab, and tons of other economically important marine species. Lance Trasky, a former Alaska Department of Fish and Game biologist, wrote an article in 1982, titled, "Kachemak Bay - the richest bay in the world?"

Today, the marine life has declined. No longer are shrimp and king crab fished commercially; salmon runs are artificially enhanced; Steller sea lions are on the threatened species list and many scientists think harbor seals should be; harlequin ducks, Stellers eiders and murrelet numbers are down; murres and kittiwakes are not reproducing as successfully as in former years; and Kachemak Bay boaters see fewer whales. These declines in marine life are not unique to Kachemak Bay. Many coastal communities witness the same perplexing population losses and no one really knows why. But, the friendly folks, the natural beauty and the fascinating prehistory and history remain.

Homer is easily accessible by commuter airlines with several daily 45-minute to 60-minute flights from Anchorage. Once in town, numerous private companies offer airplane or helicopter flightseeing trips over Kachemak Bay, the Harding and Grewingk-Yalik icefields, or to remote locations. McNeil River State Game Sanctuary, 100 miles west, is accessible by floatplane from Homer. Visitation to the coastal brown bear sanctuary is based on a lottery system. The island volcano of Augustine looms as an alternate destination for those heading to McNeil.

The Alaska Marine Highway System and numerous national and international tour ships dock in Homer.

The Seward and Sterling highways connect Homer with other peninsula communities and with Anchorage, a five-hour scenic drive. Until the early 1950s when the Sterling Highway was made passable, local beaches served as roadways at low tide. Collectors of coal and many Russian residents who live at the head of Kachemak Bay still use the beaches for travel.

Celeste Fenger, executive director of the Homer Chamber of Commerce, says that within five years tourism could be the leading industry in Homer. Off-season activities are being developed. A king salmon fishery, harvesting feeder kings wintering in Kachemak Bay, is luring fishermen to Homer, and birdwatching for finches, raptors, several species of eiders and loons, plus hundreds of bald eagles, fed by the "Eagle Lady," attracts birdwatchers. The "Eagle Lady," Jean Keene, lives near the end of the spit and

Early residents cut blocks of ice from Kenai Lake for their winter's water supply. (Helen Rhode)

feeds eagles scraps gathered from nearby fish processing plants. About 60 species are documented during the annual Christmas Bird Count; 234 are on the local checklist, including a nesting pair of common yellowthroat spotted in tall marsh reeds near the McDonald's in downtown Homer. Dr. George West, a former zoophysiology professor and administrator at the University of Alaska Fairbanks who has retired to Homer, is spearheading an effort to have Mud Bay at the base of Homer Spit included in the Western Hemisphere Shorebird Reserve Network. The network calls attention to the critical nature of a chain of major shorebird habitats in North America, Central America and South America. The Fox River flats at the head

The late Cecil Rhode, long-time peninsula resident, ice fishes at Upper Jean Lake. Rhode was born in North Dakota in 1902 and raised in Kansas and Oregon. During his youth, he was a watchmaker and tinkerer. During the Depression of the 1930s, he went to Hollywood because he wanted to make movies. In 1933 he was working in California's Feather River country when he met an old-timer who had been in the gold rush at Nome. The old-timer told Rhode and his brother Leo that Alaska was the place to be. The brothers picked olives that spring, and drove a Model T to Seattle where they bought steerage to Ketchikan. There Cecil traded a rifle for a rowboat and rowed to Haines. He worked seasonally at various jobs for the Civilian Conservation Corps, for the U.S. Forest Service, as a construction worker and as a miner for the Alaska-Juneau Mine in Juneau and for other outfits. Cecil also made several attempts to float the Yukon River, drawing other members of the Rhode family north for these efforts. During his adventures, he continued taking photographs, which he showed to employees at Boeing Aircraft Co. where he worked during World War II. He met his wife, the late Helen Powell Rhode, at Boeing, and after the war the two of them came to Alaska, to a cabin he had built on the shores of Kenai Lake in the 1930s. At this time Cecil expanded his photography and became a famed cinematographer. The couple's films and photos achieved world-wide recognition. Cecil died in 1979, Helen in 1992. (Courtesy of David Rhode)

of Kachemak Bay is the other area on the Kenai Peninsula for which this designation is sought.

Coastal currents temper Homer's climate. Mean temperatures in January are 20.7 degrees, in July 60.2 degrees, making outdoor activities possible and comfortable all year. A mere 25 inches of rainfall produce lush summer greenery and outstanding gardens but gray coastal days are common.

After the flurries of summer, Homerites switch gears for winter. Many residents support environmentally safe businesses in contrast to the strong pro-oil and gas development attitude found on the upper peninsula. Homerites voted to be a nuclear-free community several years ago and, every winter, residents go to bat for one cause or another. A few years ago townsfolk mobilized to forestall oil leases in lower Cook Inlet. More recently they successfully fought proposed logging on the south side of

Late summer fireweed colors a landscape of homesteads and farms along North Fork Road inland from Anchor Point. (David Rhode)

Kachemak Bay, and urged the state to buy Seldovia Native Association lands and add them to the state park. Commerce in the Homer area sometimes comes down to the quality of life versus the Big Buck.

Homerites support more than 50 non-profit organizations so off-season includes a host of bazaars, fund-raising events and monthly programs postponed during summer. Cross-country skiing, ice skating and snowmobiling replace summer activities and the traditional Winter Carnival dispels deep-winter blues. Kachemak Bay Branch of the University of Alaska Anchorage resumes classes, and continues planning for an expansion because the single-building campus no longer meets the needs of an increasing enrollment.

A strong visual and performing arts community exists in Homer. Woodworkers, weavers, jewelers, potters, painters and quilters exhibit their wares in numerous galleries and studios. Traditional performing arts activities include the Nutcracker ballet, the Messiah, a wearable arts show, Pier One Theater performances and the Spring Arts Festival.

Homer is an exciting, enticing city. In the words of one of its best-known residents Tom Bodett, entertainer and national radio personality, residents and visitors find life good "at the end of the road."

Anchor Point

By Janet R. Klein

Commercial fishermen, fishing and hunting guides, homesteaders and many small business owners call Anchor Point home. The 1,500 people who reside in the unincorporated community and surrounding hills and the tens of thousands of summer visitors find basic commodities and services here: two grocery stores, a post office, two restaurants, gas stations, a video shop, an automotive repair shop, several tackle shops, a motel, several bed and breakfasts and other enterprises. Just 12 miles north of Homer or 60 miles south of Soldotna, Anchor Point residents are within easy reach of whatever else they might need.

As elsewhere on the peninsula, fishing is the key attraction. Alaska State Parks manages the Anchor River State Recreation Area that encompasses five campgrounds, four along the Anchor River with its popular fishing holes. About 135 campsites, RV parking and easy access lure fishermen all summer as does the annual King Salmon Derby. Privately owned RV parks and camping areas abut the park. Custom fishing charters are available and small boats can be launched directly into Cook Inlet from the beach for hooking halibut or saltwater salmon.

A sign, at the end of the Sterling Highway spur, acknowledges the westernmost point on the contiguous North American road system.

Fishing is becoming a year-round attraction on the lower peninsula. King and silver salmon, Dolly Varden, rainbow trout and numerous other species are available throughout the summer and, when cottonwood leaves turn golden along the river bottom, steelhead fishermen appear to stand in solitary, often frosty silence, for the chance to catch and release a 3-pound to 15-pound fish full of fight. In winter, a saltwater king salmon fishery is attracting off-season fishermen who can't resist just one more fishing trip.

Seeking the Northwest Passage in 1778, British Capt. James Cook sailed northward along the Kenai Peninsula and lost a large kedge anchor at a point just south of the present-day community, giving Anchor Point its name. Before then, the area was known as *Layda* (*Laida*) to the Dena'ina.

Individual gold seekers panned the beach gravels and stream outlets in the 1880s. When Homer Pennock and his Alaska Gold Co. crew arrived in 1896, they concentrated water into a lengthy ditch and sluiced for gold near the mouth of the Anchor River. Not enough was recovered to warrant further exploration.

Several hardy individuals and the Granroos family settled on the wooded plateau in the late 1890s. About 50 years later, a religious group and homesteaders arrived and, slowly, a community grew. In 1945 Sherman and Vi Chapman homesteaded 160 acres of what is now the center of Anchor Point. Other families followed. A handful had already filed on acreage along the river or below the bluff on the beach. To earn income, the Chapmans and many others worked at the Port Chatham Packing Co. cannery at Portlock, a now abandoned settlement on the peninsula's outer coast.

A community landmark, the Anchor River Inn, began in part in one of the cabins built by the homesteaders. Joe and Elizabeth Aprill opened the business, but sold to Bob and Julie Clutts, who began the expansion that has led to the inn's prominence today.

Today, an active Chamber of Commerce provides direction to community development. Hoping to expand and diversify tourism, residents of the southern peninsula are considering the construction of a volcanic observatory between Anchor Point and Ninilchik. Such a facility could provide a dramatic look at recently active peaks such as Redoubt and Augustine. With ideas, inspiration and active citizens, Anchor Point will continue to grow in popularity.

ABOVE: *The community of Anchor Point straddles the Sterling Highway at its westernmost point. About 1,500 people live around Anchor Point, but thousands more descend on the community in summer. The large Anchor River State Recreation Area located here has campgrounds fronting Anchor River and Cook Inlet. (Jim Lavrakas)*

LEFT: *Famed Kenai Peninsula trapper and miner Harry Johnson became well known for his wildlife photographs, which he made into pastcards. In this undated photo, Johnson stands outside his cabin on Abernathy Creek between Kenai Lake and Hope. Johnson died in 1965 at age 90. His cabin is being nominated for the National Register of Historic Places. (Helen Rhode)*

Hope and Sunrise

By L.J. Campbell

The small town of Hope, northernmost community on the Kenai Peninsula, started out as a lively gold camp in the late 1890s. Today, this quiet burg on water's edge is an end-of-the-road retreat for an assortment of old-timers, grubstake miners, history buffs, a big-game guide, gold nugget jewelry makers, some teachers, highway workers and a handful of amiable business types.

Hope sits at the foot of tall mountains at the mouth of Resurrection Creek, on the south shore of Turnagain Arm. The Hope Highway to town cuts north off the Seward Highway to follow Six-Mile Creek to the shore.

The town has become a jumping off spot for adventurers today, just as it was a rendezvous point for prospectors 100 years ago. With water on one side and national forest on the other, Hope has good salmon fishing, wilderness hiking, bicycling, river rafting, whale and seal viewing and gold panning.

Several popular trails start around Hope. The historic Resurrection Pass Trail between Hope and Cooper Landing ascends 19 miles through mountains to Resurrection Pass before continuing to the Kenai Valley. The trail picks up again at the Russian River Campground, where it is known as the Russian Lakes Trail, and continues to Cooper Lake and on to Seward. Many people hike the trail in summer. It is used by skiers and snow machiners in winter. At the end of the Hope Highway, the forest service's Porcupine Campground overlooks the water. From here, the scenic Gull Rock Trail follows an old wagon trail parallel to Turnagain Arm.

Hope's new gold mining museum and several gift shops, restaurants and lodges offer diversions for those wanting to stay closer to town. Its rustic buildings

FACING PAGE: *Downtown Hope, population about 200, maintains its rustic atmosphere despite modern influences. The social hall, near right, dates back to 1902. Down the street stands the town's first general store, built in 1896 by George Roll. It now houses the Seaview Cafe. Many people in town still remember the building's second owner Iver Nerhus, a Norwegian druggist and gold miner known around town as "Doc Nearhouse." The faded "Nearhouse General Store" sign still hangs on the front of the building. Nearhouse's store overflowed with eccentricities. One person recalls a glass case displaying a head of lettuce beside a woman's necklace. Men's stiff collars from the early 1900s could be found on the shelves 40 years later. Nearhouse kept about 30 cats that had the run of the store, and were often found napping on produce in apple and orange crates. His nephew Robert Twait visited Hope in 1952, stayed and married Carla Clark, a daughter of old-timers Carl and Emma Clark. Today the Twaits raise exotic birds in Hope. Nearhouse died in 1962. (David E. Trask)*

RIGHT: *Kayakers play in whitewater on the East Fork of Six-Mile Creek. This is one of Alaska's most beautiful and popular whitewater streams with challenging rapids, deep canyons and a fantasia of waterfalls. The East Fork is easily reached by the Seward Highway. (Steve McCutcheon)*

Only a few timbers from old buildings mark the abandoned townsite of Sunrise City, once a bustling gold-mine town on the northern peninsula near Hope. (David Rhode)

and laid-back atmosphere speak of times past.

Because Hope is off the main highway, it does not get big busloads of tourists. The people who visit Hope are, for the most part, resident Alaskans or self-guided tourists in rental cars and motor homes.

The people who founded Hope were a self-guided lot, too. They were looking for gold in a largely unmapped territory. The Russians did some prospecting on the Kenai Peninsula in the early 1850s, finding a few specks of color. The first reported American gold find on the peninsula occurred about 1888, when Alexander King paid off debts in Kenai town with gold he had panned from northern peninsula streams.

This sent local prospectors scurrying. Charles Miller filed the first claim on Resurrection Creek, near where Hope would rise. Gold was also discovered on Six-Mile Creek. Finds on Bear and Palmer creeks soon followed. Gold seekers fanned through the region, prospecting any trickle into Resurrection or Six-Mile creeks. Claims on Lynx, Mills and Canyon creeks in the Six-Mile drainage became hot property.

In July 1895, miners in the Six-Mile Creek area formed the Sunrise Mining District and started the town of Sunrise City. The next year, miners in the older Turnagain Mining District, which included Resurrection Creek, started Hope City. The two towns were about nine miles apart.

At its height, Sunrise was larger and wilder than Hope, perhaps because there was more activity along the Six-Mile, perhaps because it had two saloons while Hope was allegedly dry. But nothing is left of Sunrise City today. The land is privately owned and a few people have built homes there. Fires took most of the town in the early 1900s and a lone remaining warehouse floated away into Turnagain Arm after the 1964 earthquake.

It is unclear exactly how many miners came into the mountains around Hope during the 1896 gold rush. A generally accepted estimate is about 3,000 men, although some histories say twice that. Carl Clark, who came to Hope in 1913, has always maintained that there were no more than 1,500 in Sunrise at its peak and 500 in Hope. Most of the prospectors came by boat into Cook Inlet, landing at the supply towns of Tyonek or Knik for forays up Susitna River or into the Turnagain District. Some came by boat into Prince William Sound and crossed Portage Glacier onto the peninsula. Still others came into Seward, following and prospecting streams along their way overland. Boat traffic on Turnagain Arm was heavy during this time, despite the arm's enormous tides, as small steamers shuttled men and supplies.

Few of the miners found the fortunes they sought. Some did handsomely, able to stash a small nest egg. Most worked for wages on someone else's claim and left the area after a few seasons to try their luck elsewhere.

One story credits a group of miners for naming Hope to match their outlook. A more common version says the town was named for Percy Hope, the youngest in a group of about 100 prospectors who landed in 1895.

Sunrise's name apparently came from its location. Albert Weldon "Jack" Morgan, a placer miner out of Sunrise from 1897 to 1901, wrote about the naming of Sunrise in his memoirs, recorded many years later when he was 92: "There was a high mountain on the southeast side with two very sharp peaks that stood away up high. When the sun came up in winter, it was low enough to go behind one peak for awhile and come out for a short while, and then go behind the other until it got past it. That made three sunrises, and that was why the town was called Sunrise."

By summer of 1897, Hope had about 80 people while Sunrise had about 150. The next summer Sunrise became, for a short time, one of the largest towns in the territory with about 800 people. Many of the miners left during the winter.

Morgan stayed in Sunrise during winter 1898, along with a dozen married couples and 50 to 60 bachelors. Sunrise had three general stores and two big log saloons where "the boys would loaf and play cards there late." That winter, the Sunrise miners built an entertainment hall with a dance floor and a stage for locals inclined to theatrics. People from Hope would come on Saturday nights to dances, with music provided by whoever brought instruments.

Hope had its own entertainment hall, built about 1902 by Edwin Crawford and Al Davis out of

In 1988, Hope celebrated the centennial of the first American gold discovery on the northern peninsula. This find triggered a rush of prospectors, and those who mined Resurrection Creek founded Hope. The weekend festival was put together by the town's women. The opening night, shown here at the social hall, included singing, a recitation contest of Robert Service poetry and awards for best gold-rush costumes. (David Rhode)

Flowers bedeck the historic Carson cabin in Hope. Prospectors Passwater and Carter built the cabin in 1896, hauling logs to the site with a bull. Miner and postmaster Elmer Carson made the cabin his home and post office in the 1930s. Later owners Rosa and Gene Buttedahl set about preserving the cabin and cultivated big gardens around the place, selling lettuce to Anchorage restaurants. After the 1964 earthquake, Barbara and Art Anderson bought the property and continued gardening in colorful displays. (Penny Rennick)

whipsawed lumber. Today the hall is used for meetings and community parties. Each July, the Hope 5-K Run starts here. The women raffle a handmade quilt as part of a weekend bazaar.

"We all love the social hall," says Ann Miller, who retired in 1991 after serving as Hope's postmistress 26 years. Miller remembered that people from all around would come to dance on Saturday nights, and the children would be lying on benches along the walls asleep. Vera Wolfe, the wife of former Moose Pass postmaster, Delbert Wolfe, said she could remember dancing down into a hole where the floor had sunk, then back out.

After the 1964 earthquake, Hope residents lifted the building, and replaced the timber foundation and floor. In the 1980s, the interior was sandblasted to reveal unusual three-sided logs.

As a gold mining supply town, Hope also had a couple of stores. One was an Alaska Commercial Co. outlet. The other store was built in 1896 by George Roll with finished lumber shipped up from Seattle. Roll imported apple trees to plant around his store, giving Hope a novel product for several decades.

"There are a lot of historic buildings left here," says Don Ohr, owner of the Seaview Cafe, Bar and Motel. "If you're coming to Alaska to see the lifestyle of the late 1800s, you'll find it in the town of Hope." Ohr and his partner Joyce Baldwin came to Alaska from Montana in 1981 on a visit that never ended. They kept returning to Hope that summer and ended up leasing the main street business. They only operate in summer because the pipes freeze in winter. Ohr drains and disconnects the plumbing each fall, storing the pipes under the buildings until the next spring. The couple also runs a year-round towing service.

Don co-authored *A Place Called Hope* (1986) with writer and former Hope resident Donna Grundman. This slender history includes recollections of miner Carl Clark. He was 5 when his family moved to Hope in 1913. Clark and his wife Emma were the oldest old-timers in Hope until recently, when they moved. The people of Hope speak of them in reverential terms.

Hope may be a rustic-looking place, but that is its appeal, say some of the people who run businesses along the road and in town. A new Chamber of Commerce is promoting the town's gold rush history, and the Hope Historical Society is excited about opening the Hope and Sunrise Mining Museum in summer 1994, a project 25 years in the planning.

Hope outlasted Sunrise, perhaps because a few

miners continued having success. Among them was John Hirshey, who had arrived in 1895 and struck finds on Bear Creak, Coeur d'Alene Creek and finally, in 1911, opened what became one of the best-paying mines in the district, the Lucky Strike Mine above Palmer Creek south of town.

The town had a brief resurgence in 1914, when three taverns opened to entertain railroad construction crews. In May 1918, the Sunrise post office closed and the mail from Seward went on directly to Hope. By 1930, Sunrise had only two miners.

Gold mining ceased during World War II, and Hope dropped to only about 50 people. Carl Clark started doing big game guiding, later turning over his area to William Miller. Two or three sawmills opened and closed during these years. The 1964 earthquake dropped the town's waterfront four to six feet, and the townspeople moved a number of buildings to higher ground. Electricity came to Hope in 1967, and telephones a few years later. These modernizations, along with a large new school built during the last decade, helped the town slowly grow to its current population of about 200 people.

A number of individuals still do mining out of Hope. They hold small claims and make enough to live on when gold prices are right, say locals. These grub-stake miners come to town periodically, checking in with businesses like the Discovery Cafe, Henry's One Stop and Bear Creek Lodge for telephone messages.

Some Hope residents have combined gold mining and tourism. Barbara Wright and Mel Hislop of BJW Mining and Gifts, make jewelry out of local gold and let visitors pan for gold in their front yard.

The only commercial gold mining company working area claims today is the Hope Mining Co. The company holds gold mining leases on about 2,800 acres of Chugach National Forest, says company president Al Johnson, an Anchorage mailman. This company descended from the Mathison Mining Co.

started by Robert B. Mathison and his three sons in 1899. Carl Clark owned the company at one time, and it was purchased by the current owners in 1973.

The Mathisons helped spur the gold fever that gripped the area by finding 386 ounces of gold in 59 days of placer mining, according to Ohr's book. After nine years of mining by hand, Mathison raised money in 1906 from outside investors to buy hydraulic equipment, to mine more ground faster.

Today, gold fever still haunts Hope, along the streams where miners stomp, in the cafes where locals spin stories, in the eyes of newcomers chasing a claim. "We always have young people coming in," muses Miller, "thinking they are going to find it."

A salmon fisherman finds an unusual moment of solitude at the mouth of Resurrection Creek near Hope. A section of this creek farther upstream is open to the public for recreational gold panning. (Danny Daniels)

As important as fish and fishing are to the lifestyle and economy of the Kenai Peninsula, it seems surprising that only one community can point to fishing as the impetus for its initial founding. Halibut Cove on Kachemak Bay's south shore is that lone child of the Kenai fishing industry.

Halibut Cove

By Janet R. Klein

Sheltered in the eastern corner of Kachemak Bay, about six miles from Homer, is Halibut Cove. Glaciated, 4,000-foot peaks of the Kenai Mountains shelter the cove from storms brewing in the Gulf of Alaska; and Kachemak Bay State Park and Wilderness Park provide a 368,000-acre backyard playground.

Cove residents are intimately linked with the sea. Their community name, bestowed in 1880 by scientist and explorer William Healy Dall, honors the tasty bottomfish that frequent Kachemak Bay; and from 1911 to 1928 a herring fishery flourished here. Salteries, perched on pilings along the shoreline, ringed the cove and seasonal workers, especially Scots and Scandinavians, were imported to pack the unusually large herring for export to the West Coast and Midwest. Today, the large herring are gone and

From the Sea

LEFT: *Six acres of vibrant blue buoys, floating above a network of sunken lines, identify the first experimental oyster farm in Halibut Cove. (Janet Klein)*

FACING PAGE: *Halibut Cove, a small, eclectic community of about 80 people, mostly fishermen and artists, is located about six miles across Kachemak Bay from Homer. The cove, served by passenger ferry from Homer, is a popular tourist retreat for summer visitors to Kachemak Bay. (Charlie Crangle)*

only remnant pilings remain of the former fruitful fishery.

Many cove residents are commercial, sport and subsistence setnet fishermen who catch salmon.

Kachemak Bay inspires cove residents, in the kitchen and in their studios. Salmon, halibut, cod and, on rare occasions, shark entice seafood lovers to Halibut Cove to dine at The Saltry, its only restaurant. The dozen or so resident artists depict sea life on their canvasses, ceramics and jewelry. Artist Diana Tillion takes a more direct approach in bringing the marine environment to her art. She uses octopus ink to paint her canvasses.

The present community of Halibut Cove began shortly after World War II. Although a few bachelors remained after the herring boom, it was young men, such as Alvin (Slim) Taeschner and Clem Tillion, who settled and reared families. Almost 50 years later, they still call the cove home.

TOP LEFT: *For several years artistic renditions of Alaska Natives in various groupings have greeted visitors to The Saltry, the well-known seafood restaurant at Halibut Cove. (Penny Rennick)*

ABOVE: *Halibut Cove patriarch, Clem Tillion has been active in fisheries politics for decades. His crusades on controversial issues helped shape policies on fisheries taxation, management and allocation. Tillion, originally from New York, came to Halibut Cove in 1947. The cove had boomed with herring fishermen in the 1920s, but was practically deserted when Tillion arrived. He recruited fishermen, artists and skilled laborers to move there. He fished commercially for salmon and halibut, but voluntarily divested to avoid conflicts with his political fisheries posts. While in the state legislature, 1962 to 1981, he supported creation of a state park surrounding the cove. He and his wife, Diana, an artist, raised four children at their home in the cove on Ismailof Island. Today, Tillion remains involved in fisheries issues, most recently as a top fisheries advisor to Gov. Walter Hickel. (David Rhode)*

Halibut Cove in winter is quiet and secluded. With no public facilities, the 20 or so permanent residents are self-sufficient. Freezers and cupboards are stuffed with fish, garden produce, clams, moose meat and berries. A mail boat makes twice weekly runs to Homer, weather permitting, and the two elementary-age children are schooled at home.

The cove bustles in summer. The population swells tenfold and tourism and art-related businesses reopen and flourish. Thousands of visitors wine, dine and shop here from Memorial Day to Labor Day, most arriving from Homer via the *Danny J*, which has plied local waters for 28 years. A wooden boardwalk, several art shops and studios, and tantalizing forest trails invite visitors to explore the western end of Ismailof Island. Floatplanes tie up at the public dock on the eastern end of the island, and helicopters buzz overhead on flight-seeing trips to nearby Grewingk Glacier. Where once commercial fishing was the economic mainstay, today, tourism and art prevail.

Halibut Cove has reached a pleasant place in its evolution. The hustle of summer is offset by the solitude and serenity of winter.

LEFT: *A northeast storm on Kachemak Bay pounds the thin isthmus between the two parts of Ismailof Island. (Cross Fox Photography)*

BELOW: *A hiker surveys the northern edge of Kachemak Bay State Park, which surrounds Halibut Cove on the landward side. (Cross Fox Photography)*

The Good Earth

Homesteading has been a part of the Alaska myth for nearly a century. The lure of a big land, filled with 160-acre parcels that could be claimed with hard work and a little luck, encouraged World War II veterans to head north. This influx of former soldiers and others seeking a new life led to the founding of Soldotna and Sterling.

Soldotna

By Janet R. Klein and L.J. Campbell

Soldotna, one of the youngest towns on the peninsula, began when the spruce- and birch-covered lowlands and lake country along the Kenai River were opened to homesteading in 1947. A preference given to World War II veterans enticed bachelors and young families to the area and, slowly, a settlement began.

Some consider the town's name a derivation from the Russian word *soldat*, meaning "soldier." Others suggest that it arose from a Dena'ina word that meant "stream fork."

Today, the first class city stretches more than a mile along the Sterling and Kenai Spur highways.

LEFT: *Quick growth in the young town of Soldotna has led to pockets of residents and businesses scattered among the forests of the lower Kenai River valley. In late winter when the willow shoots of the previous year are buried in snow or already eaten, moose visit Soldotna in search of food. (Ron Levy)*

FACING PAGE: *Transportation and commercial hub of the northern peninsula is Soldotna, strung out along the Sterling Highway at a bend in the Kenai River. One of the town's businesses, an elegant restaurant formerly called the Four Seasons, recently caught the attention of the famous New York restaurant with the same name. The Soldotna restaurant has changed its name to Through The Seasons. (Steve McCutcheon)*

Soldotna area residents will celebrate summer 1994 with two rodeos, one near Memorial Day Weekend and a second rodeo in conjunction with the city's Progress Days festival at the end of July. (Lance Peck/Picture Library Associates)

Soldotna's location at the junction of these roads helped it become the business center and supply headquarters for the upper peninsula, an area encompassing some 20,000 people. The neighboring communities of Sterling, Ridgeway and Kalifornsky particularly rely on Soldotna and the attachment is unlikely to wane. Several national retailers have selected Soldotna as the site of their first outlets on the Kenai Peninsula: Safeway and McDonald's line the western side of the Sterling Highway, and a Fred Meyer has opened on the east side.

Located about 150 highway miles, or a three-hour drive, southwest of Anchorage, Soldotna borders the Kenai National Wildlife Refuge. Refuge headquarters and visitor center, south of downtown, provide information on fishing, boating, camping, hunting, photography, hiking and other outdoor opportunities available on the refuge's 1.9 million acres.

Soldotna is largely a government town, as well as a service center. In addition to the federal wildlife refuge offices, several branches of state government are located here, including divisions of the Alaska Department of Fish and Game and the peninsula headquarters of the Alaska State Troopers. Soldotna is also the seat of the Kenai Peninsula Borough government.

A number of Soldotna's approximate 4,000 residents work in the petro-chemical industries headquartered in Kenai and Nikiski. The Swanson River oil strike in 1957, Alaska's first significant oil find, brought a boom to Soldotna. Some of the early homesteaders remember seeing oil field workers in the downtown cafe a few days before the strike was announced; they knew something was up by the stains of black goo on the men's overalls.

"After oil was discovered, it was a totally different picture. We had to move over and make room for all the families that came in," said Marge Mullen. She and her husband, Frank, a former Air Force pilot, homesteaded Soldotna in 1948. She has retired from running a restaurant in Soldotna and among other things today, conducts a community class about Soldotna's history. "The oil development happened so quickly," she recalls. A pilot and two heavy equipment operators — Sterling homesteaders Jesse Robinson and Morris Coursen — marked the route for the Swanson River Road to the oil field by air, dropping toilet paper on the treetops as they flew over, she recalls.

Oil excitement was soon followed by discovery of a large gas field a few miles west of town. Soldotna was the first town on the peninsula that tapped natural gas for heating and cooking.

Soldotna was rapidly incorporated as a fourth-class city in 1960, but it took four elections before residents voted to upgrade to first-class status in 1967, giving it power to levy property taxes.

The Kenai Peninsula College came to Soldotna in 1963, to a campus located between Soldotna and Kenai. Today, the fully accredited division of the University of Alaska Anchorage offers two-year degree programs and a popular vocational tech program. Its 1,800 students come from all over the peninsula.

Soldotna also has the regional hospital serving the upper peninsula. Kenai wanted the hospital, but several doctors had homesteaded in Soldotna where it was eventually built.

Fishing for salmon on the Kenai River is the prime visitor attraction in Soldotna. Many fishing guides, boat rentals, tackle shops and other support businesses are easily found in town. Bed and breakfasts are sprinkled along the shores of the meandering Kenai River upstream and downstream from the bridge at Soldotna, with the potential for a salmon dinner just a fishing line's throw away from the front deck. Each summer, the Soldotna Silver Salmon Derby offers more than $12,000 in cash prizes to anglers. As befitting the city that calls itself the "sport fishing capital of the Kenai Peninsula," resident Les Anderson caught in the Kenai River the world record salmon on sport tackle — a whopping 97-pound, 4-ounce king.

The early Soldotna-area homesteaders — people like Frank and Marge Mullen, Jack and Margaret Irons, Jack and Dolly Farnsworth, Howard and Maxine Lee, Larry and Rusty Lancashire — juggled a

Clear waters of the Moose River enter the Kenai River at Sterling. The bridge across the river has since been widened as part of a road improvement project through town. (Steve McCutcheon)

variety of jobs to make ends meet. Some fished commercially and worked in canneries, some worked construction in Anchorage, the Lancashires and Mullens tried farming but had to work other jobs too, and some worked in construction on the Sterling and Kenai Spur highways.

Today, these roads are paved arteries clogged with traffic in summer. But when the homesteaders arrived, these roads were barely cleared trails pockmarked

Soldotna's main business district flanks the Sterling Highway from this bridge over the Kenai River to the junction with the Kenai Spur Highway, about a mile northeast. This part of town has boomed during the past decade with new construction of fast food franchises and a big mall along the highway. (Jim Lavrakas)

with mud holes. Stories of early travel have become part of Soldotna's folklore.

Katherine Parker relates several such stories in her chapter about Soldotna in Walt and Elsa Pedersen's *A Larger History of the Kenai Peninsula* (1983). Take the time Dewey Magee started hiking to Kenai from his homestead east of Soldotna. He came upon Hal Thornton returning to Kenai, stuck in the mud in his Jeep. Dewey helped him out of the mud, and Hal offered him a ride on to Kenai. "No thanks," said Dewey, "I'm in a hurry."

The first car made its way over the highway into Soldotna the next year, in 1948. Loren Stewart brought his new Oldsmobile from Anchorage by train to Moose Pass, then spent two days driving the 64 miles to Soldotna. Stewart spent much of that time stuffing branches and logs into mud bogs to get across, Parker writes.

There's even a road story attached to first homestead baby in Soldotna. Dolly Farnsworth flew to Anchorage to give birth to daughter Linda, then flew back with her baby to Kenai, where husband Jack met them in an old truck for the drive to Soldotna. The truck's engine quit partway home in the bitter cold. As Jack tried to restart it, Dolly huddled with her newborn, frantically trying to warm the baby's bottle by holding it under her arm. "It was a rough trip people tell about to this day," said Parker recently.

The first grocery was opened by Don and Verona Wilson in 1952. The grocery joined a small cadre of businesses, a service station and garage, sawmill and concrete block plant and the Bear Den Bar. Soldotna's first homesteader, bachelor Howard Binkley, was the first to subdivide his riverfront property down by the highway bridge, and this became the town's core residential district. The Farnsworths and the Mullens owned property around the highway junction, the "Y" as it's locally known.

These homesteads became the heart of the town's

ABOVE: *Ken's Alaskan Tackle, a Soldotna landmark, has a scale where anglers weigh their big Kenai River salmon. (Jim Lavrakas)*

RIGHT: *Jennifer Nickles holds up a string of rainbow trout caught in the Swanson River system on the Kenai National Wildlife Refuge. (Jon R. Nickles)*

business district along the highway from the Y to the Soldotna bridge. A central town square was never platted, so the town developed in hodgepodge fashion in a strip along the highway, sometimes called ironically "The Miracle Mile."

"When we first came here, we could see just a few lights down below. Now there's a myriad of lights," says Parker, who homesteaded one of the last 40-acre parcels with her husband, Charlie, in 1961. She wrote for the local newspaper and he surveyed land. Now retired, they still live at the top of their homestead hill above the busy highway junction. "I like country living, but I like the convenience too. I think it's easier to shop here than Anchorage." They operate Parker's

Map Shop at the end of their driveway and have seen more foreign tourists each year, particularly Germans, who are in town to fish.

Today, tourism is increasingly important in Soldotna. Some 25,000 people register each year at the Kenai refuge visitor center. Throngs of people from Anchorage visit Soldotna each summer, but the city gets its share of the peninsula's out-of-state tourists, too. The out-of-state guests spend nearly $9 million a year in just the Soldotna-Kenai area.

Several public campgrounds and parks are located in Soldotna along the river. The river downstream from the bridge gets particularly heavy use. More

A fisherman nets a king salmon on the Kenai River. The river is famous for trophy-sized kings, but is also known for its red and silver salmon, trout and Dolly Varden. (Al Grillo)

banks are to start at Soldotna Creek Park in 1994 and at Centennial Campground in 1995. Visitors should stay out of posted areas where new plantings are taking root. With these projects, Soldotna is the first public landowner along the Kenai to do something about bank erosion and loss of fish habitat caused by crowds of shoreline anglers.

The Kenai River Festival in early June celebrates the river with music, the first fresh red salmon of the year, puppet shows, and a juried arts and crafts exhibit. And the festival swims with salmon of the two-legged kind; in one of the tents, children paint and stuff big salmon hats to wear around the grounds. The festival includes booths and displays by agencies and groups involved with the river, to educate the public about what is needed to keep the river healthy. The festival was started in 1990 by a handful of environmentalists concerned about the river's future and is now sponsored by a recycling group, said Peggy Mullen, a homestead daughter, city council member and founder of the first festival.

There are, of course, things other than fishing to do in Soldotna. Some local people, in fact, hardly wet a line anymore, put off by the crowds of tourists. Others look to the river for birdwatching, kayaking and canoeing. Summer days, long as they are, are still too short to satisfy all the outdoor possibilities. The town's Progress Days, including a parade, rodeo and dance held each July, allow residents and visitors an opportunity to enjoy the exuberance that overtakes Alaskans in summer.

Snow machining into the hills, ice skating, skiing, hunting and bingo help pass the long winter.

The Kenai Peninsula Visitor Information Center, operated by the Soldotna Chamber of Commerce, distributes information about the upper peninsula. The center is located, appropriately, on the banks of the Kenai River, immediately west of the Soldotna bridge. Local attractions include the Soldotna

than a dozen fishing guides operate private camps and charter services on the river's bend below the bridge, north of the city limits.

Several popular state recreation sites on the river are reached from Soldotna, off the Kenai Spur or Kalifornsky Beach roads. These include Slikok Creek, Big Eddy and Ciechanski state recreation sites.

Three city recreation areas on the river — Swiftwater Campground, Soldotna Creek Park and Centennial Campground — stay packed during summer. Projects to revegetate badly damaged river

Historical Society Museum with a wildlife display and a historic log village that includes early homestead cabins and a territorial school house. Soldotna also has a nine-hole golf course. The Central Peninsula Sports Center, with an Olympic-sized ice rink, resounds with local hockey players. The sports center also has racquetball and volleyball courts, a running track, a weight and exercise room and convention facilities.

Soldotna is depending increasingly on tourism, and like other peninsula communities, it is developing off-season activities. With thousands of residents on the upper peninsula alone and another 200,000 plus from Anchorage only a 30-minute flight away, Soldotna is seeking to entice more Alaskans to enjoy its fishing, boating, wildlife watching and culture.

A number of tiny settlements, such as Crooked Creek, Cohoe and Happy Valley, dot the Sterling Highway along Cook Inlet between Soldotna and Homer. About 80 people live in Clam Gulch, centered around the post office and lodge shown here. (Jim Lavrakas)

Sterling

By L.J. Campbell

Homesteading in the late-1940s brought about the community of Sterling, a wide spot on a lonely pioneer road through the central peninsula forest.

The wide spot then was called Naptowne. Its single business was the Naptowne Inn, a restaurant and gas station owned by Alex and George Petrovich, brothers from Indianapolis who adopted that city's nickname for their enterprise. The Naptowne post office opened in 1949.

But in 1954, the homesteaders renamed their community Sterling, for Hawley Sterling of the Alaska Road Commission. They had grown tired of "sleepy" jokes about Naptowne, so the story goes, and circulated a name-changing petition at a celebration of the Sterling Highway's official opening through town. The signatures flowed as freely as the booze. "There are still a lot of old-timers around who'd like to get it changed back to Naptowne," says Les King, owner of the Naptown Trading Post. He inadvertently dropped the "e" when he bought the business 14 years ago.

Today, the Naptown Trading Post is a modern twist on the past, a convenience mart with everything from ammunition to videos. It operates in a new building, because bulldozers leveled the original structure to widen the road.

The old road through Sterling didn't get a lot of traffic at first. It was dirt and gravel between the towns of Kenai and Seward. Homesteaders used it for hauling supplies and, almost as often, landing their planes. "The road was the homesteaders' salvation," said Elsa Pedersen, a homesteader, writer and editor of several peninsula histories. The road provided construction jobs for the settlers and gave them a way to bring in goods. Today the Sterling Highway is the central and western peninsula's main artery.

In 1957, an oil strike along the Swanson River north of Sterling put the community on notice. Homesteaders thought Sterling would grow as an oil field service town, because it was the closest settlement. Hoping oil was under their properties, many of them signed long-term leases. After several years without drilling, the homesteaders sued the oil

This modern thoroughfare replaced three miles of the old narrow Sterling Highway through the community of Sterling. The 126 sodium vapor lights along the road brighten the sky through winter, day and night. Some local people objected to the project's scope and $6.7 million price tag. Others grumble that the streetlights have ruined their view of the aurora borealis. Others in Sterling praise the highway, saying it will bring new businesses to town. (Jim Lavrakas)

A controlled burn was set to encourage secondary growth of browse species for enhancement of moose habitat, part of an effort by the U.S. Forest Service in the late 1970s and early 1980s. (Charlie Crangle)

company to vacate the leases. Meanwhile, oil did bring people, jobs and new businesses, but most of them went to Soldotna and Kenai, towns down the road with bigger landing strips and a port for receiving oil field supplies.

More recently, the people of Sterling fought successfully to close a dump on a hill above town that received drilling mud and other hazardous oil field wastes. The borough oversees periodic monitoring of the site, which remains a possible source of contamination.

As it has turned out, Sterling's wealth flowed past its doors, instead of under the ground. Its location on the north bank of the Kenai River, at the mouth of the Moose River, gave homesteaders prime riverfront access to world-class salmon fishing.

Walt Pedersen was one of Sterling's first homesteaders, when it was still Naptowne. In 1947, he operated a flying service to locate land on the peninsula for homesteaders. A forest fire had raged through the central peninsula that summer from Hidden Lake, near Cooper Landing, west to Soldotna. By fall, when rains extinguished the blaze, most of the forest and muskeg held only charred skeletons of trees and ankle-deep ash.

But Pedersen recognized the potential of Kenai River property, and homesteaded at the mouth of the Moose River, a placid tributary where he could land a floatplane. He and his first wife, Laura, built the Moose River Resort. He later developed his property north of the resort into a residential subdivision where he and his second wife, Elsa, still live. According to Pedersen, his was the first tourist resort on the Kenai

ABOVE: *Sue and Glenn Simpson float among lily pads while on a trip through the Swanson River canoe system. (Helen Rhode)*

TOP RIGHT: *Homemade rafts as intriguing as the Loch Ness monster cruise along the Moose River each July during the Moose River Raft Race. (Ron Levy)*

River. Now called the Great Alaska Fish Camp, it is operated by Pedersen's daughter Kathleen Haley and caters to fishermen from outside Alaska.

Today, the highway through Sterling is dotted with tourist-related businesses — several fish camps and outfitters, a bed and breakfast, a motel, several RV parks, gas stations, two auto parts stores, convenience marts, a couple of restaurants, a greenhouse and a tool rental shop.

The Izaak Walton State Recreation Site, with campsites, picnic tables, toilets and a boat launch, is located in Sterling below the Moose River highway

bridge. Sterling also accesses the Swan Lake canoe trail in the Kenai National Wildlife Refuge. Canoe rentals and bus shuttles to the trail's put-in point are available here.

Every July in Sterling, local businesses sponsor the Moose River Raft Race, now in its 13th year. Racers paddle homemade rafts down the river to the cheers of locals and tourists on the banks.

According to the 1990 census, about 3,800 people live along the rivers, streams and lakes in the woods around Sterling. But that covers too broad an area, say locals who peg the population nearer 2,500. Sterling has a number of absentee landowners from Anchorage who own cabins along the Kenai River and show up in summer to fish.

The community has an elementary school, five churches and a senior citizens center that features bingo games and rents out as a social hall. A number of small service businesses operate out of homes, off the main highway.

In many ways, Sterling is a bedroom community of Soldotna, the next larger city 12 miles west. A lot of

Sterling people work, shop and bank in Soldotna, and Sterling students attend junior high and high school there. This dependence has stunted attempts to make Sterling more of a retail center. A big grocery and a bank opened, then closed, in Sterling several years ago. A mini mall stands empty. Sterling also had a fish processing plant that employed about 40 people, which also has closed.

However, Sterling does have the peninsula's largest furniture store, which draws customers from all over.

Sterling is unincorporated with no local government. This suits the independent-minded and outspoken folks who live here. Yet some of them think Sterling needs something akin to a community council, a collective body composed of local people to voice community priorities to the borough, state and federal governments.

"We definitely have our work cut out for us," says Dennis Merkes, 34, a Sterling resident spearheading this grass roots effort. His parents, Grace and Leon, homesteaded in Sterling when he was an infant. "There are a number of people here adamantly opposed to any type of organization. They don't want to be represented, to have anyone claiming to represent them, and I definitely understand this. But the place is growing so fast, we have to have a say in what's happening. I'm absolutely not advocating any more government, just a local voice of the people to make the government we have be more responsible to us.

"If we don't, we'll be washed away and slowly eroded with no place to stand...our pioneer spirit taken away by default."

Merkes points to renewed discussions about the state building a highway bridge from Sterling across the Kenai River to open up more land along the Funny River Road. This 13-mile gravel road from Soldotna runs on the south side of the Kenai River, and it dead-ends at the river opposite Sterling. The community should have a say in what happens here, Merkes says.

In 1994, Sterling got a new five-lane stretch of highway through the middle of town. It was designed to handle summer's heavy traffic more safely than the shoulderless strip it replaced. The $6.7 million road — with sidewalks, curbs, gutters and bright lights — has been controversial. Some residents believe it will encourage growth and new businesses. Other say the money was needed in other places. They worry that traffic will now speed through Sterling, only to find dangerous bottlenecks at each end where the highway narrows back into two lanes.

In any case, the new big-city thoroughfare has made Sterling an even wider wide place on the road.

The Killey River heads in the glaciers of the Kenai Mountains and flows northwest 32 miles to join the Kenai River. (Ron Levy)

Offspring of the Railroad

The early 1900s brought a flurry of railroad construction to towns on Alaska's southern coast. Each wanted to build the first railroad to the Interior, an All-American route to the gold fields. Only Seward on the Kenai Peninsula succeeded.

Roads came with the railroad, and the settlement of Moose Pass grew with construction of both.

Seward

By L.J. Campbell

The historic town of Seward sprawls beneath mountains at the head of Resurrection Bay.

Seward is the only town on the southeastern coast of the Kenai Peninsula, and it has become a springboard for ocean adventure and maritime commerce. Its deep-water port off the Pacific Ocean stays busy year-round with a mix of fishing boats, pleasure craft, freighters and ocean-liners. It is linked by the Seward Highway and the Alaska Railroad to the state's biggest city, Anchorage, a few hours to the north.

LEFT: *Wind-hardened snow dapples the convoluted surface of Exit Glacier in Kenai Fjords National Park. A paved trail goes to within one-quarter mile of the glacier's face before splitting into a lowland trail and a steeper one up the side of the glacier. Mountain goats can be seen on steep slopes and black bears roam the lower woodlands. Visitors should heed warning signs and not approach too close to the glacier because falling ice can cause injuries. (Richard Montagna)*

FACING PAGE: *Communities all over the Kenai Peninsula celebrate summer with various festivals. A parade kicks off the annual Fourth of July celebration in Seward, which draws people from throughout southcentral Alaska. Its main event is the Mount Marathon Race. (Danny Daniels)*

Coal goes onto a ship at Suneel Alaska Corp.'s coal loading dock in Seward. The Alaska Railroad carries ore from Usibelli Coal Mine at Healy, near Denali National Park, to the Seward terminal for export to Korea. The state dredged the port and built the dock in the 1980s, at a cost of about $5 million, to aid development of the state's coal resources. (Jon R. Nickles)

Seward started in 1903 as a railroading town, one of Alaska's earliest planned communities. As such, it played an important role channeling people and goods north and westward into Alaska from cities outside.

Two brothers, John and Frank Ballaine from Seattle,

promoted Seward as the ice-free ocean port for the Alaska Central Railway. They arrived on a ship with about 80 others anxious to help build the new town. The Resurrection Bay Historical Society Museum in downtown Seward has artifacts and photographs of early Seward. Author Mary Barry includes numerous anecdotes and profiles the town's founders in her two volume set, *Seward Alaska, A History of the Gateway City* (1986 and 1993).

Four years and 53 miles of railroad track later, Seward was booming. Among other things, it had a daily newspaper, the *Seward Gateway*, an important source of outside news for the region. But the Alaska Central was bankrupt.

A new company, the Alaska Northern Railway, bought the line and extended the track to mile 71 on Turnagain Arm. Promoters lost interest and stopped construction when the federal government closed Alaska to coal claims, halting development of mines in the Matanuska Valley that the railroad had been trying to reach.

In 1914, the federal government chose to build its own railroad to open Alaska's minerals and agriculture. The railroad commission decided to run the government line from Seward to Fairbanks, and bought the barely functioning Alaska Northern.

With this, Seward became the tidewater terminus for an overland route to the Interior, an achievement coveted by several other towns with railroad projects of their own, including rival Valdez on Prince William Sound.

During its early years, Seward gained another distinction. It became the gateway to the Iditarod gold fields, the coastal end of a trail through the Alaska Range and on to Nome. The trail, promoted by the Seward Commercial Club and developed by the Alaska Road Commission, served as a mail route to Iditarod from 1914 through 1919.

Prior to Seward's founding, other groups occupied Resurrection Bay at different times. The early Natives included Alutiiq speakers, the Unixkugmiut, who lived on the peninsula's coast. One of their villages,

An Alaska Central Railway crew poses with the train's wood-burning engine. The Alaska Central was the original railroad out of Seward, the reason for the town's founding in 1903. Promoters planned to lay track to the Interior, but completed only 53 miles before going bankrupt in 1908. Two years later, the line was purchased by the Alaska Northern Railway, which extended track to Turnagain Arm. In 1915, the federal government bought the Alaska Northern for the southern leg of its railroad to Fairbanks, which became today's state-owned Alaska Railroad. (Courtesy of Steve McCutcheon)

This photo looks north along 4th Avenue in downtown Seward sometime after prohibition ended in 1933. The historic Brown & Hawkins Corp., shown on the left side of the street, still operates here today under Hawkins family ownership. These original buildings, constructed in 1904 and 1908, now house Brown & Hawkins, Bob's Market and a mini-mall. Another historic Seward business, Urbach's Clothier, operates across the street today. Leon Urbach opened his store in 1915, and now his son, Larry, runs it. (Courtesy of Michael Nore)

Kuta-Krq, was located near where Seward is today. Another village, Kanilik, was also thought to be nearby.

For the most part, the Russians overlooked Resurrection Bay during their forays, perhaps because its entrance was hidden by rocks. The exception was one small, but significant, installation.

In 1792, Alexander Baranov set up a ship-building yard in Resurrection Bay. Baranov managed the Shelikov-Golikov Co., the dominant Russian trading company in Alaska. Owner Grigorii Shelikov wanted to bolster the company's achievements to impress Russian royalty and get a trading monopoly. He also needed to squelch advances elsewhere on the Kenai Peninsula by the rival Lebedev-Lastochkin Co.

Baranov employed English ship-builder James Shields, but had little in the way of supplies other than nearby timber. They invented what they lacked. For metal, they gathered iron scraps washed ashore from shipwrecks and added iron ore mined on the peninsula. Forest moss mixed with hot tar became caulking. Tar was made from spruce gum and oil. Tar and whale oil mixed with red ochre from iron deposits became paint. Colored canvas pants were sewn into sails.

Despite a mutiny by the shipwrights, raids by the rival company and threats from angry Natives, the Resurrection Bay shipyard produced the first sailing vessel built in Alaska. The *Phoenix*, a 180-ton, 73-foot frigate, was launched in August 1794. The Russians had little subsequent use for Resurrection Bay and abandoned the post shortly afterward.

The third period of modern human activity came in 1884, in the persons of sailing Capt. Frank Lowell and his Alutiiq-Russian wife, Mary Forgal, from English Bay. They landed as Mary was about to give birth. They homesteaded and raised nine children here. Fur buyers, explorers, government geologists and gold prospectors visited them. Frank sailed off in 1893, leaving Mary and the children, some married and living on nearby homesteads. The Lowell land became the core of Seward.

Today, Seward probably approaches what its founders envisioned. It is a small, self-contained, energetic community of about 3,000 year-round residents. Yet its port, railroad and paved highway make it a gateway into Alaska for thousands of people and tons of cargo.

Seward is busiest in summer, when tourists come to town. It's a favorite destination for people out of Anchorage, many of whom drive down to fish and boat in Resurrection Bay. Travelers also come into Seward off the Alaska Marine Highway. The ferry *Tustumena* home ports in Seward and stops several times a month during summer on a route that includes Valdez and Kodiak. It uses the city's Fourth Avenue dock on the south end of downtown.

The city expected 94 cruise ships to visit in summer 1994. The number of cruise ships into Seward has steadily increased since the first one stopped in 1982. The cruise ships use the railroad dock north of downtown. Some of these passengers only glimpse Seward from the waterfront as tour guides quickly route them onto trains or buses for the next leg in their tour of Alaska.

Seward's business community would like these passengers to spend more time in their city, shopping and touring downtown. The city is developing additional visitor attractions to help it become more of a destination.

A big project in that direction is a proposed $46 million Alaska SeaLife Center on the downtown waterfront. Its promoters say the center will be a premiere marine research and rehabilitation facility with a visitors center and sea life aquarium. It would be built adjacent to the state university's existing marine research institute that opened in 1969. The state has agreed to fund $12 million of the project. Another chunk of money will be forthcoming from the 1989 *Exxon Valdez* oil spill settlement. Promoters hope to complete fund-raising and have the new facility under construction by 1995.

As it is, Resurrection Bay's scenery and wildlife draws thousands of people each summer for

Runners scramble up a rocky chute during the Mount Marathon Race, held each Fourth of July since 1915 in Seward. The record time to run up and down the 3,000-foot mountain was 43 minutes, 23 seconds, set in 1981 by Bill Spencer. (Charlie Crangle)

When fishermen come into the harbor at Seward to clean their catch, they attract Steller sea lions, which feed on the scraps. These marine mammals have suffered a drastic population decline in recent years, and are currently listed as threatened under the Endangered Species Act. (Lance Peck/Picture Library Associates)

Marathon and the water, the downtown still serves as the community's main shopping and business district with stores, restaurants and bars that stay open year-round. The heart of downtown includes a historic district with several early buildings, such as the architecturally noted Swetman House and the town's oldest inn, the Van Gilder Hotel. St. Peter's Church dates back to 1905, the peninsula's first protestant church.

Brown & Hawkins Clothing, Gifts and Souvenirs occupies its original storefront, built by partners C.E. Brown and T.W. Hawkins when the town started. The men were Klondike gold prospectors who went to Nome, then Valdez where they operated a general store. Hawkins accompanied the Ballaines on the ship to Seward in 1903 and by the next year, he had convinced partner Brown to move their business to Seward. Both men became prominent figures in business and politics.

Hawkins daughter, Virginia Hawkins Darling, owned and operated the store for 30 years. In 1990, she sold the store to son Hugh Darling and his wife Iris, who moved to Seward from Florida. Virginia still works at the store each day. She owns two adjacent buildings that were part of the original department store that now house a grocery and a small shopping mall.

The store still has some original fixtures, including a floor-to-ceiling ladder that rolls along a track and an old cash register. The building even lasted through the 1964 Good Friday earthquake that destroyed much of downtown. "There's not a level floor in the place," said Iris, chuckling. "You leave a rack of clothes out at night and there's no telling where it will have rolled by the next day."

Seward's downtown waterfront includes a public park with 300 spaces for recreational vehicles and tents. On the north end of downtown, the city's busy small boat harbor sports a boardwalk lined by restaurants, boat charter kiosks and specialty shops.

sightseeing. Several tour companies offer day-long excursions out of the bay into the waters of Kenai Fjords National Park. Some of these include round-trip train passage from Anchorage.

Those who spend some time in downtown Seward will find the same orderly layout platted by its founders. Snugly tucked between the flank of Mount

Bardarson Studio is one of the only shops in the boat harbor that stays open year-round. This gallery features works by Alaska artists and Alaska-made gifts. Owner artist Dot Bardarson calls Seward "the town that smiles" and "nature's playground."

After all, the downtown beach and the harbor docks are good places to watch curious sea otters watching back.

On the Fourth of July, downtown offers any number of places — if the weather is clear — to watch the Mount Marathon Race. From downtown, the runners look like a moving dots as they race up and down the 3,000-foot mountain behind town.

The first official race was held in 1915, although Sewardites had been dashing to its peak for years. Before the town had a communications cable to the outside, people used to wager on the arrival time of steamships. Crafty bettors would dash up the mountain to spot the ships in the outer bay, then race back to make their bet.

Today, men, women and children scramble over near-vertical slopes of loose shale, ice patches and snow fields as they try to best the race's record time of 43 minutes, 23 seconds set in 1981. Scrapes, cuts and bruises come with the territory, battle scars best seen up close by crowds at the finish line. The field of 800 is composed largely of Anchorage runners who test their mettle against the mountain in return for T-shirts, patches and free showers. The winners get trophies. The winner of the first race got a suit of clothes.

Fishing is big in Seward, from shore and from boat, for pleasure and for pay. Seward is particularly known among sport fishermen for its big silver salmon and halibut. Each summer, some 5,000 people buy tickets in Seward's Silver Salmon Derby that starts the second Saturday in August. The ticket-holder catching the biggest silver wins $10,000. The record fish to beat: 19 pounds, 14 ounces caught in 1992. The city's halibut derby runs through the month of July. A 300-pound

Land (bottom) and sea otters are frequently seen at Seward, a center for marine studies in southcoastal Alaska. (David Roseneau, below; Harry M. Walker, bottom)

halibut is not uncommon, says Cyndy Dickson with the Seward Chamber of Commerce.

Commercial fishing supports the town, too. Four fish processors have facilities on the bay. They compete with transient fish buyers for the local fleet's catch of salmon, halibut, herring, cod and a small amount of shrimp and scallops. The processors hire college students to work through summer's salmon runs, and tent communities spring up outside the plants.

Fishing is practically a year-round industry, yet the commercial fleet represents less than half of the 3,000 vessels using the city's small boat harbor annually. Most of the users are recreational boaters. Seward's scenic location and easy access make it an increasingly favorite harbor with Anchorage boat owners, who comprise about 60 percent of the users.

A typical day in summer brings some 900 boats to the harbor, built for many fewer. Demands by recreational boaters and fishermen for more moorage has driven a decade of discussions about building a second boat harbor. In 1994, Al Schafer, owner of Afognak Logging, a general construction firm in Seward, was negotiating to develop a private small boat harbor on city tidelands east of town, off Nash Road.

Nash Road cuts off the Seward Highway north of the airport and leads around the bay to Fourth of July Creek on the shore opposite downtown. The road goes to the Marine Industrial Center that opened in 1984. The Seward shipyard with its 250-ton travel-lift for boat haul-outs and repair is located here, as is Seward Forest Products, a sawmill producing lumber for shipment to Asia.

The city is actively pursuing more industries, touting its deep-water, ice-free port, rail and highway

connections. "We need industry to keep us going through the winter," said Iris Darling, president of the Chamber of Commerce.

Seward's economy includes a prison, a coal loading facility and a large vocational school. The Spring Creek Correctional Center, a maximum security center on Nash Road, employs several hundred people. Suneel Alaska Corp. operates a coal transfer facility, where coal from Healy in the Interior is loaded onto

Seward is the jumping-off point for excursions to Resurrection Bay and Kenai Fjords National Park. This excursion boat is exploring a black-legged kittiwake colony in Resurrection Bay. (Danny Daniels)

ships for Korea. The Alaska Vocational Technical Center, which opened in 1969 as the Alaska Skills Center, has facilities spread throughout town, from dorms in the residential areas to shops in the industrial section on the town's north end to classroom buildings at the foot of Mount Marathon. The center employs about 65 people and offers 31 different training programs, ranging from mechanics and welding to culinary arts and coast guard officer licensing.

Seward has experienced slow growth the past several decades. Its early years were marked with ups and downs. Construction of the Alaska Railroad, along with both world wars, brought people and jobs, then lulls.

In 1925, the Jesse Lee Home, an orphanage operated by the Methodist Church, moved to Seward from Unalaska in the Aleutian Islands. Benny Benson, the boy who designed Alaska's Flag in 1927, lived here. The home was moved to Anchorage in 1966.

During World War II, Seward became the site of Fort Raymond. After the war, several military buildings were converted to other uses, including a tuberculosis sanitarium. Today, the Forest Acres subdivision occupies part of the original fort site; the remainder holds the Seward Military Recreation Camp.

In 1963, Seward received an All-American City award, the second smallest city so honored. Then the Good Friday earthquake of 1964 basically shut down town. The waterfront slid away. Waves washed back into town, adding flooding to the fires and destruction. About 95 percent of its industry was lost. The city rebounded, getting its second All-American City award the next year.

It was three years before the railroad dock, an important piece of the town's commerce, was rebuilt. Meanwhile, the railroad had transferred much of its cargo business to Whittier. The dock sat idle until the late 1970s, when construction of the trans-Alaska pipeline brought shiploads of 48-inch pipe to Seward for transport north by rail.

It seems that President Warren G. Harding's description of Seward, made in 1923 during his visit to open the railroad, would still apply today: "A rare jewel in a perfect setting."

LEFT: *Downtown Seward snuggles at the foot of Mount Marathon on Resurrection Bay, where it started in 1903 as a railroad town. The small boat harbor, north of downtown, stays busy with fishing and pleasure boats. The railroad dock, to the right of the harbor, handles cruise liners in summer and serves as a log loading facility. The 1964 earthquake destroyed much of Seward's waterfront including the railroad dock, which was later rebuilt. Resurrection River flows into the bay at the top of the photo. (Jon R. Nickles)*

FACING PAGE: *This brick student Services Center in downtown Seward is part of Alaska Vocational Technical Center, which serves 225 to 300 students daily. (Rex Melton)*

A large crowd gathers along the Seward waterfront in mid-January for the annual Polar Bear Jumpoff. The icy plunge into Resurrection Bay, a fundraiser for the American Cancer Society, attracts a wide range of hardy, costumed characters who jump for charity pledges. (Charlie Crangle)

Moose Pass

By L.J. Campbell

The early forging of trails and rail through the peninsula spurred settlement of Moose Pass, north of Seward.

From a single roadhouse built in 1909 to serve miners and road crews, Moose Pass grew into a railroad construction camp and section station.

The community of Moose Pass sits at mile 29 of the Seward Highway, on the southern edge of Upper Trail Lake in the heart of the Kenai Mountains. The highway brings heavy traffic to Moose Pass in the summer. The Moose Pass Inn, the Trail Lake Lodge and Motel and the Estes Brothers general store do brisk business with visitors to the many nearby streams, lakes and trails, as well as those passing through to Seward. Local youngsters earn extra money in summer by selling firewood and cookies from roadside stands.

The Alaska Railroad serves the community in summer, stopping as needed for passengers.

Moose Pass is also becoming popular in winter with people who like to ice fish, ski and snow machine.

Moose Pass has about 80 residents, according to the 1990 census. They are an interesting mix of old-timers and newcomers, Democrats and Republicans, opinionated folks who speak their minds and volunteer a lot of time to their community.

The Sportsman's Club, a civic group, has long served as the social and political backbone of Moose Pass, an unincorporated town with no local government. The club started in 1947 in a Quonset hut, then raised money to build the existing community center housing the public library and volunteer fire department. The community center, post office and elementary school are located on a side road off the main highway.

The club sponsors a Summer Solstice Festival each year and funds many other community and youth activities. The group also represents the community in dealings with the borough government. Sometimes discussions of Moose Pass include smaller communities along the highway, such as Primrose, Lakeview, Lawing and Crown Point with another 300 people. The Moose Pass volunteer fire and first responder coverage extends throughout this greater Moose Pass area.

Poke around the Moose Pass town site, and it is easy to find its history.

Ed Estes, owner of Estes Brothers store in the middle of town, is a Moose Pass fixture. He is 82 and has been here since 1921, when his stepfather, Frank Roycroft, took a job as Moose Pass section foreman for the Alaska Railroad. His mother, Leora, became the first postmistress, officially naming the town. Neither Roycroft or Oscar Christensen, owner of the original roadhouse, wanted it named after them, so she adopted the name from a mountain pass across the

The community of Moose Pass snuggles into a crook of Upper Trail Lake, nearly six miles long. (Penny Rennick)

lake where moose hung out. The family operated a sawmill in Moose Pass during the 1930s, one of several in the area that produced lumber for homes and railroad ties. In the late 1930s, Ed carried mail by dogsled from Moose Pass to Hope. The family also operated a waterwheel that provided electricity to the community until the 1950s.

Today outside the store, a waterwheel still works, turning a grindstone. The message on the sign next to it reads: "Moose Pass is a peaceful little town. If you have an axe to grind, do it here." Estes wryly calls his store the "only non-profit grocery on the peninsula."

"I might get it on a paying basis one of these days," he says, adding that business picks up in summer. "I'm a damn fool for doing it, but a little place needs a grocery store."

A popular visitor attraction just north of Seward is Exit Glacier off the Seward Highway. Trails lead through alder-covered moraines to a spot near the face of the glacier. (Danny Daniels)

One of the oldest buildings today in the town is the Moose Pass Inn, according to owner Wes Sherrill Sr. The inn was originally built in the 1930s. At various times under different owners it housed the post office, a grocery and roadhouse with rooms to rent. Today, Wes and his wife, Linda, operate a restaurant and package store, with a liquor license dating back to territorial days.

On the other side of the road sits the Trail Lake Lodge, a new-looking log affair that dates back to the mid-1940s. It used to be the Jockey Club, a restaurant that in its prime was one of the finest on the peninsula. In 1989, Jeanne and Ken Follett bought and renovated the lodge, restaurant and a nearby motel, which had been standing vacant and badly deteriorated.

"We took the town eyesore and made it into something the town can be proud of," said Jeanne.

Their efforts were helped along by the *Exxon Valdez* oil spill cleanup. The Exxon Corp. was looking for inexpensive housing on the peninsula for its community service employees, who were sent to help businesses that had lost workers to the high-paying cleanup jobs. Exxon reimbursed the Folletts for repairs to the motel needed to get it open quickly.

More recently, the couple has vigorously advertised the lodge as a winter recreation headquarters, to supplement the summer tourist season.

Other Moose Pass businesses include TAK Outfitters with horseback trips in summer and guided snow machine trips in winter; Scenic Mountain Air floatplane and flight-seeing service, which also instructs and rates floatplane pilots; the Alaska Railroad section station with a resident maintenance crew and track inspectors; and the Trail Lake Fish Hatchery operated by Cook Inlet Aquaculture.

Moose Pass area residents have spent long hours charting the future of their community, and they developed a land use plan to guide its growth. Moose Pass is encircled by state land, which can be

A waterwheel runs a grindstone outside Estes Brothers store in Moose Pass. The attraction sports some practical advice for small-town living — if you have an axe to grind, do it here. (Harry M. Walker)

transferred to the borough for community use as dictated by the land use plan. Residents were looking forward to putting their plan into place. In spring 1994, they were dismayed to learn that the state land around Moose Pass, some 7,000 acres, might be transferred to a private Mental Health Lands Trust as part of a proposed court settlement. They strongly oppose this land going into private ownership because the community would have no room to grow and could be surrounded by uncontrolled, incompatible development, said Ann Whitmore-Painter, chairwoman of the Moose Pass Advisory Planning Commission.

River of Dreams

By L.J. Campbell

The Kenai Peninsula is a fishermen's Eden. The fish are big and swim within easy reach. The peninsula's rivers, lakes and miles of coastal waters teem with record-size salmon, trout and halibut. Some of the world's finest sport fishing is found here.

Anglers come from many countries to cast their lines into the emerald waters of the Kenai River for trophy king salmon. They stand shoulder-to-shoulder on its tributary, the Russian River, for red salmon. Boats crowd the beaches near Deep Creek and Anchor River and the harbors at Seward and Homer. They target halibut and salmon in Cook Inlet, Kachemak and Resurrection bays. Sport fishing guides and charter boat operators charge hundreds of dollars a day for their services and find people eager to pay, booking reservations often months in advance.

The peninsula's fisheries have grown ever more popular during the past two decades. There seems to be no end to the demand for more fish. But the popularity packs a price. Battles over allocation of the resource between user groups are common. Regulations used to manage these sport fisheries have become increasingly complex as more and more anglers compete for a limited resource. Some of the peninsula's fishing streams are at risk of being loved to death.

● ● ●

Sport fishing's modern odyssey on the Kenai Peninsula starts in large part with the Kenai River and

LEFT: *Sun glints off scarlet highbush cranberries on the slopes above Kenai Lake, headwaters of the Kenai River. This view from near the northwestern end of the lake looks southeast to Porcupine Island. (Chlaus Lotscher)*

FACING PAGE: *Brenda Masuda cradles a 50-pound king salmon caught on the Kenai River. (Al Grillo)*

Granddaddy of the peninsula's rivers is the Kenai, which flows west about 80 miles from Kenai Lake to Cook Inlet at the town of Kenai. Kenai Lake was an important travel corridor until 1938, when missing segments of the central peninsula's roads were completed. People traveled by dog sleds, horses, trucks and cars across the frozen lake in winter; in summer, taxi-boats ferried people between Cooper Landing, Lawing and the lake's southern tip, which met the road from Seward. (Helen Rhode)

its trophy salmon. This river has produced 19 world record salmon. Among them, the world's largest king, a 97-pounder, now hangs mounted on the wall at the visitor's center in Soldotna.

The Kenai River is an 82-mile natural spectacle. It starts in a glacier-fed mountain lake, pools through another lake, plunges in white-water, winds through lowlands and mixes at its mouth with saltwater tides from Cook Inlet. Eagles, bear, moose and caribou,

along with thousands of migrating ducks, geese and cranes, depend on the river. Some 27 species of fish swim its water. Glacial silt suspended in the water gives this stream its intense green color, and each bend of the river flows into another photo opportunity.

What sets the Kenai apart, though, is its number and size of salmon. Nature has endowed the Kenai with two runs each of king, red and silver salmon, instead of the typical single run. This means more salmon are migrating into fresh water during a longer period of time, giving fishermen more weeks to fish. For some reason, its salmon are larger than those in other rivers.

These big fish draw crowds. The Kenai is the state's most popular salmon stream. Its giant kings made it famous in the 1970s, and then anglers discovered the river's abundant red and silver salmon. The equivalent of 332,000 anglers fished the Kenai in 1992, some 100,000 more than the decade earlier. A typical summer morning can find more than 2,000 of them in the 10 miles below Soldotna, with as many as 50 boats per mile churning the water.

Humans have distinguished the Kenai in another way — making it one of the easiest rivers to fish in the world. The access comes as roads, waterfront camps and parks, motels and resorts, public and private boat launches and docks. Roads lace the peninsula and the main east-west artery, the Sterling Highway, parallels the Kenai for most of its length. Good fishing is often just a short walk or boat ride away from a roadside pull-off. The Kenai River, as well as the peninsula's other fisheries, are within a few hours' drive of 70 percent of the state's population. This is unusual since trophy sport fishing most anywhere in the world involves expensive flights to remote, wild rivers.

Yet the lower Kenai River is hardly wild or remote. It passes through four communities including the peninsula's largest towns, Soldotna and Kenai. Urban sprawl of homes and businesses flanks much of its lower half. More than 66 percent of the riverfront property below Skilak Lake is in private hands. The rest of it is in public ownership. Little of the river's banks are in protected status, and there are few ordinances governing their use. Development along the Kenai occurs basically unrestricted.

"We're supposed to manage the river to provide recreation and preserve and protect it for fish and wildlife," says Chris Titus, manager of Alaska's state parks on the peninsula. The Kenai River in 1984 was designated a special management area under state parks. Titus grapples daily with Kenai River issues.

"It's almost conflicting, to manage it that way. The ideal habitat for salmon would be no development and no use, but we don't live in that world. The Kenai is a popular place to recreate and own property, and we can't blame people for having their dream to live on the Kenai River and fish their property. But we have plenty of examples from the Lower 48 where people have developed land along salmon streams and the river has died," Titus says. "If we succeed, the Kenai will be one of the few rivers with urban development that can maintain healthy salmon runs."

"There are those who feel," she adds, "that the Kenai River is nearing the crisis stage."

The lower Kenai River is plagued by heavy boat traffic, shoreline development and bank trampling by fishermen. All this contributes to loss of vegetation and habitat important for fish survival and reproduction. There are concerns about pollution — hydrocarbons washing into the river from roadside storm drains, potential toxic spills from highway river bridges, fecal contamination from people using the banks as a bathroom.

In addition to worries over the river's biological condition are political questions: who should be able to use the river, conditions and limits of that use, and allocation of fish harvests. There are a myriad of conflicts between users — non-guided fishermen versus guided fishermen, bank anglers versus boat anglers, motor boat fishermen versus drift boat fishermen, riverfront property owners versus trespassing bank anglers, and so on.

These problems have been in the making for many years and will not be solved overnight. Attempts in

The Kenai Peninsula's big moose became famous among hunters long before sport fishermen discovered its trophy-size salmon. This moose chomps a mouthful of underwater plants near Cooper Landing. (Jennifer Brannen)

the past have fallen short. Everyone seems to agree the river needs to stay healthy with fish, but no one can agree on the best way to make that happen.

• • •

Until 40 years ago, about the only people who fished the Kenai were the few folks living along its shores.

Along with plenty of fish for the peninsula's earliest people, it provided a travel route between interior and coast. During the early part of this century, homesteaders staked parcels along its shores, helping build a road that brought more settlers. The Kenai's big fish stayed more or less local knowledge until the late 1950s, when the Swanson River oil strike brought a population boom.

Local men started hiring out as fishing guides, perfecting their methods and gear for catching the giant king salmon that migrated up the river each spring and summer to spawn. News of the Kenai's big fish spread, drawing more anglers and more fishing guides.

The kings, which are caught mostly from boats, usually hang out in deep midstream channels. The early days of king fishing brought bigger boats with more powerful motors that raced along the river, shooting flumes of water into fragile banks. Land-

TOP LEFT: *A privately operated ferry carries passengers to the far bank at the confluence of the Kenai and Russian rivers. (Alaskana Photo-Art)*

LEFT: *Thousands of fishermen converge each summer at the Russian River to cast for red salmon. These shoulder-to-shoulder crowds define the term "combat fishing." Some of the heaviest fishing takes place where the Russian River joins the Kenai River. The Russian River hosted the state's top sport red salmon fishery for years, with the Kenai River's red fishery second biggest. The rankings recently flip-flopped when the Kenai River experienced record numbers of returning reds. (Ron Levy)*

Dave Morel, of Marathon, Fla. (left) and Leland Hudson, of Cottage Grove, Ore., clean fresh-caught red salmon along the Kenai River at Soldotna's Centennial Campground. (Sean Reid)

owners began to complain about the boat traffic. They were encouraged to reinforce their banks with riprap, or walls of rock.

Some of the guides began to complain, too. Their growing business was attracting fly-by-night operators, who sometimes took advance payments then disappeared. The proliferation of fishing guides also triggered worries, even among the guides, about overfishing and crowding on the river.

As the king sport fishery on the Kenai grew, so did the prestige of owning and developing a piece of the Kenai shoreline.

By the 1980s, fishery biologists were becoming alarmed that the riverbank development would harm the salmon. The edges of the river in their natural state provide important habitat for young king salmon. Native plants and woody debris along the banks give salmon fry hiding places from predators and slow down the water, providing an easier route upstream. There were studies on rivers in the Pacific Northwest showing that changes to the shoreline that eliminated vegetation or increased the water flow — such as riprap, groins and jetties — also destroyed important salmon habitat.

In 1982, the state convened a Kenai River Task Force, to look at problems on the river and recommend solutions. Two years later, the Kenai River was designated a special management unit of the state park system, and in 1986 a comprehensive management plan was adopted. Air boats were prohibited and boat motors were limited to 35 horsepower.

The plan also called for sweeping changes in how the river and adjacent uplands should be managed to protect fish and wildlife resources, recalls fishery biologist Terry Bendock, who has been involved with the Kenai River for years. But the changes called for in the river's management plan could only be regulated by the borough and local governments through zoning powers. "These measures were bitterly and successfully fought by land owners, who in most cases, wanted fewer impediments to developing the shoreline," wrote Bendock in "It's Wake-Up Time on the Kenai River, An Alternate View of Our Progress," which appeared in the May 1993 issue of *Alaska's Wildlife*, the now-defunct Alaska Department of Fish and Game magazine.

During this period in the 1980s, fishermen started targeting red salmon on the Kenai. Reds enter the river after kings, and most of the reds on the Kenai are caught in late July by fishermen along shore.

The first run of reds to enter the Kenai head into the clear waters of the Russian River, between Kenai and Skilak lakes. The Russian is as famous for its reds as

ABOVE: *Denizens of high crags on the southern peninsula, mountain goats attract wildlife watchers to the mountains around Seward and suitable slopes near Cooper Landing. Hikers in Caines Head State Recreation Area on the west side of Resurrection Bay can encounter the goats on the lower slopes in late winter. (George Wuerthner)*

TOP RIGHT: *The crystal waters of Lost Lake reflect 5,710-foot Mount Ascension in Chugach National Forest. Backpacker Marilyn Wakeland enjoys the scene from the lake's east shore, a long-popular hiking destination on the southern peninsula. Two trails lead to the lake. Primrose Creek Trail starts seven miles north in Primrose Campground, off the Seward Highway on the shore of Kenai Lake. The Lost Lake Trail starts seven miles south in Lost Lake Subdivision. The subdivision is located off the Seward Highway about five miles north of Seward. (William Wakeland)*

the Kenai is for its kings, and today has problems with crowding and bank erosion.

The Kenai River for years was considered too turbid for red salmon fishing, but fly fishermen nonetheless successfully adapted their techniques. About 1987, the Kenai began getting record returns of reds and this fishery bloomed.

Today the Kenai River has the largest red salmon sport fishery in the state. Anglers caught more than a quarter million Kenai reds in 1991. If a predicted crash in red stocks materializes in 1994 through 1996, the sport fishery may be limited.

"The fishermen, thcy get the 'red madness,' that's what I call it," says Will Josey, who has seen lots of anglers in the years he's owned land along the Kenai River. "They don't think about anything but catching those fish. One fellow, his car rolled into the river. He forgot to put on the brake, he was in such a hurry."

The booming red salmon fishery brought more problems to the Kenai. Reds hug the shoreline, where fishermen on foot chase them down. Several thousand fishermen trampling the riverbanks has increased erosion and destroyed more fish habitat.

In the past decade, fishing and boating throughout the peninsula have become big business with the famous Kenai River as the centerpiece. Sport fishing on the Kenai alone generates an estimated $44 million in guide services and related expenditures in the communities. In 1992, 275 guides operated on the Kenai, charging up to $200 for a day on the river. The guides do most of the business on the Kenai during king salmon returns, May through July, and silver

TOP RIGHT: *Homer Junior High School students and teacher Hal Neace, right, gather around a campfire at Slaughter Gulch in the central peninsula. This May 1993 outing was part of the school's unique cross-curricular program that has taken place the last three weeks of school, each year since 1987. Students choose from a dozen courses that take them outside the traditional classroom, integrating academics with practical applications. Neace's outdoor exploration unit, "For Land's Sake," included tent camping, hiking, rock climbing, journal keeping and campfire discussions. (Chlaus Lotscher)*

RIGHT: *Kayakers push off to tackle some rapids on the Kenai River. In recent years floating the river has gained in popularity, and numerous rafting outfitters have opened businesses along the river near Cooper Landing. (David Rhode)*

salmon returns in August through September.

Two thirds of the visitors come to the peninsula to fish, and there is no sign that this will wane. Each year, crowds are growing on other peninsula rivers, like the Kasilof, and at the mouth of Deep Creek with its saltwater salmon fishery.

"To a local resident, the opportunities seem boundless — guiding, equipment sales and rentals, bed and breakfasts, RV parking, camping, boat

While the Kenai River is certainly the main salmon waterway on the peninsula, other area rivers also draw fishermen. The mouth of the Anchor River, so crowded with salmon fishermen in summer, takes on the silence and colors of fall in September. Anglers fish upstream for steelhead from July through October. (Janet R. Klein)

launching and mooring..." writes Bendock. "But is the growth of tourism really benign?

"The modern day gold rush that is mining tourism dollars on the Kenai Peninsula is placing the future of this magnificent resource and the fragile economy surrounding it in jeopardy."

• • •

Managing the Kenai River will continue to be a gigantic headache. Nearly a dozen state and federal agencies share jurisdiction on the Kenai. Property owners and municipalities have their agendas, too.

A number of new efforts to address the river's biological problems are being made. For instance:

•The Kenai Peninsula Fishermen's Association, made up of Cook Inlet commercial salmon setnetters, started the King Salmon Fund. Contributions are used to preserve the river's king salmon habitat through education and restoration projects.

•Kenai River Sport Fishing Inc. helps landowners protect existing fish habitat along their shoreline and restore habitat to damaged banks, through its Habitat Protection program. It awards landowners for outstanding efforts to mitigate impacts to the river on their property. Its education campaign urges fishermen to walk in the riverbed rather than on the banks.

•In 1992 and 1993, the state division of parks interviewed Kenai River fishermen to gauge reactions to crowding and user conflicts. This Kenai River "carrying capacity" study will be used to help formulate future management.

•A study documenting the structural changes along the riverfront confirmed biologists' fears that salmon habitat along the Kenai is being destroyed at an alarming rate. It found that the lower 50 miles of the Kenai contained 82 boat launches, 221 bank ladders, 70 floating docks, 136 fixed docks or landings, 49 groins, 36 excavated canals or boat basins, and 73 private revetments of concrete rubble, tires, logs, pipe,

Fishermen in boats flock to the Kenai River during king salmon season. (Al Grillo)

blocks or chain link fence, according to Bendock.

•The Kenai Soil and Water Conservation District published the *Kenai River Landowner's Guide*. It contains a discussion of the river's ecology and recommendations for habitat-friendly riverfront treatments. In some cases, this includes redoing earlier treatments, like riprap, that were once considered appropriate.

•The state legislature in spring 1994 considered tax incentives to property owners to revegetate their shores.

•A Kenai Peninsula Borough task force formed in early 1994 to look at designating the river as an area meriting special attention within the coastal management zone, to allow the borough to zone land use along the waterfront.

•The City of Soldotna in spring 1994 launched a $1 million rehabilitation of shoreline in two city parks that have been heavily used by bank fishermen.

It is clear that finding solutions to the Kenai River's problems will not come easy or cheap. But what is learned can be applied to the peninsula's other fishing streams as the sport keeps growing. As Bendock cautions, "It is not too late for the Kenai River, but the clock is ticking and it's time to wake up."

At Play on the Kenai

By Penny Rennick

They call it a playground. If that's the case, then the Kenai has much to offer children of all ages.

Government agencies control much of the peninsula's natural resources. The National Park Service, U.S. Forest Service and U.S. Fish and Wildlife Service manage areas in the south, east, central and north parts of the peninsula; the state oversees many smaller areas in the west and south. Government oversight has meant improved recreation facilities: campgrounds, interpretive signs and access have benefited from government funds. Residents of the Kenai have taken these government upgrades, added many of their own, and are building a thriving tourism industry.

A little more than a decade ago visiting the fiord-lined outer coast of the Kenai required having access to a private boat or chartering a plane. With creation of Kenai Fjords National Park in 1980, the demand to explore the outer coast spawned several tour boat operations at Seward. These tours to Resurrection, Aialik and even Harris bays open a chapter in a history book of the Pleistocene. Today's remnants of this epoch, the glaciers, roar, groan and crack as they pulverize the Kenai Mountains. Offshore swim humpback, killer and occasionally sei and fin whales. In the Chiswell Islands, part of the Alaska Maritime

LEFT: *Dean Osmar, 1984 Iditarod Trail Sled Dog Race champion, trains sled dogs along trails outside Soldotna. Osmar, a commercial fisherman, lives in the Clam Gulch area. His son, Tim, is a regular Iditarod competitor. (Ron Levy)*

FACING PAGE: *This visitor-use cabin is hidden among the birch and aspen forests of Caribou Island in Tustumena Lake, largest on the Kenai. Hunters and trappers have cabins along the lake's shore, because traveling on the water is much easier than bush-whacking through the forests. The 24-mile-long lake is reached by road off the Sterling Highway near Kasilof. (Ron Levy)*

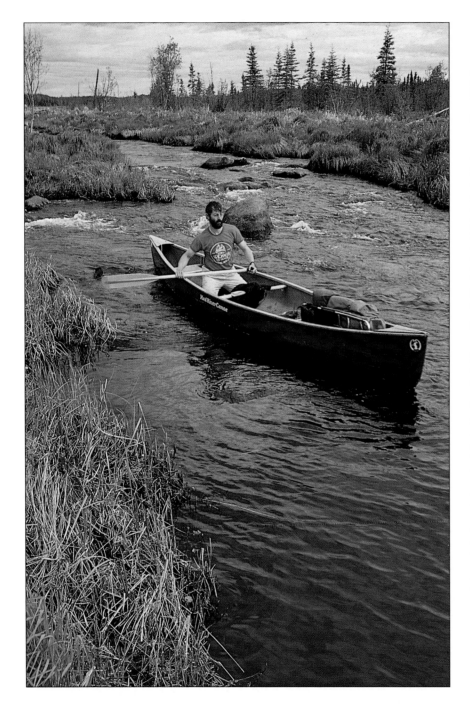

Mike Wiedmer negotiates a small rapids on the Swanson River, part of a canoe trail through the Kenai National Wildlife Refuge. This 80-mile trail connects more than 40 lakes with 46 miles of the Swanson River in the central peninsula. (Jon R. Nickles)

National Wildlife Refuge, Steller sea lions join with harbor seals, horned and tufted puffins, common and thick-billed murres, fork-tailed storm-petrels, pomarine jaegers, parakeet and rhinoceros auklets, marbled, ancient and Kittlitz's murrelets, black-legged kittiwakes, glaucous-winged gulls and red-faced, pelagic and double-crested cormorants in a menagerie of marine mammals and seabirds only 35 miles from Seward. Before the *Exxon Valdez* oil spill, the Chiswells were home to 60 percent of the nesting seabirds on the south side of the Kenai Peninsula.

On the interior side of Kenai Fjords National Park, a road has been upgraded along the Resurrection River valley and a wide trail suitable for wheelchairs has been opened to allow visitors a close-up view of Exit Glacier. A trail following the side of the glacier leads onto the Harding Icefield where adventurous and fit travelers can tackle the ice sheet atop the Kenai Mountains, most of which rise to between 5,000 feet and 6,000 feet within the park.

Much of the eastern peninsula lies within Chugach National Forest. Kenai tourists can take advantage of an expanded trail system, with routes leading usually to mountain lakes off the Seward and Sterling highways. Lost Lake, Ptarmigan Creek, Russian Lakes, Resurrection Pass, Gull Rock and Crescent Creek are popular routes into the high country through spruce, and western and mountain hemlock forests. The trail to Gull Rock is actually part of a historic route along the southwestern shore of Turnagain Arm leading from Hope to the abandoned camp at Chickaloon. A high summer ritual includes a drive to Turnagain Pass to view the wildflowers, such as wild geranium, Indian paintbrush and columbine.

Heart of the peninsula is the Kenai National Wildlife Refuge, a legacy of the national moose range that was originally set up in 1941 to protect the region's large moose and their habitat. The refuge also shelters brown and black bear, mountain goats, Dall sheep, caribou, wolves and a host of smaller mammals. The refuge stretches from the flanks of the Kenai Mountains west and north, encompassing the Caribou Hills, Tustumena-Skilak benchlands, the lakes and wetlands of the northwestern lowlands and the Chickaloon estuary. Recreationists in ever-increasing numbers fish, hunt, canoe, raft, hike, observe wildlife, pick berries, ski and snow machine in the 1.9 million acres that comprise the refuge. More than 30 percent of these lands are open only to non-motorized travel.

Refuge staff have made a concerted effort in recent years to develop a management plan that will accommodate all interests in Alaska's most used national wildlife refuge. This use has focused on the Kenai River corridor and the Skilak Loop. The 19-mile loop swings south off the Sterling Highway west of Cooper Landing, passes several lakes and campgrounds including Skilak Lake, one of the largest on the peninsula, and rejoins the highway before it reaches the town of Sterling. Numerous lakes and trails encourage boating, hiking, wildlife watching and

TOP RIGHT: *William Wakeland surveys a cross-country route through the snowy slopes of Turnagain Pass recreation area in Chugach National Forest. (William Wakeland)*

RIGHT: *Several new or renovated resorts have been added to the peninsula's visitor accommodations list and as tourism increases, more are likely to be opened. Princess Tours opened the Kenai Princess Lodge in 1990 on a bluff overlooking the Kenai River at Cooper Landing. The lodge is open from mid-March through December and offers sleigh rides in the winter. (David Rhode)*

ABOVE: *A common loon displays for visitors to Camper Lake on the northern peninsula. (William Wakeland)*

RIGHT: *A red-necked grebe sits on its nest amid lilies and aquatic vegetation. The Kenai lowlands are home to abundant waterfowl. The Kenai, Swanson and Chickaloon rivers nurture swans, loons, grebes, ducks, geese and many species of shorebirds. (Tim Van Nest)*

studies of wildflowers and berries in season. Many campgrounds are designed for families and those with limited mobility. In winter this area attracts cross-country skiers.

North of the highway, the Kenai lowlands stretch north and west to Cook Inlet. When glaciers scoured this area, they left behind numerous pockets that have filled with water, creating a chain of lakes that attract waterfowl and canoeists. The Swanson River route, 80 miles and 40 lakes, and the Swan Lake Trail, 60 miles and 30 lakes, allow paddlers to travel quietly through prime wildlife habitat, listening to the calls of common loons, reflecting on the grace of the continent's largest waterfowl, the trumpeter swan, gazing about warily for black bear and fishing for rainbow trout. To the north on the Chickaloon estuary, thousands of migrating waterfowl pass through each spring and fall. The estuary and Chickaloon watershed is the major waterfowl migratory staging area on the peninsula.

The Kenai River is the most heavily fished in the state and its upper section above Skilak Lake, a stretch known as Kenai Canyon, is one of the most frequently floated in Alaska. Included in the 240 miles of designated and maintained trails within the refuge is the Funny River horse trail, a route that winds nearly

21 miles to benchlands southeast of Soldotna.

The state manages several recreational sites along the Cook Inlet side of the peninsula, ranging south from Captain Cook State Recreational Area to Kachemak Bay State Park and State Wilderness Park. In between are numerous state-managed camp-grounds and recreation sites designed to help Alaskans and visitors enjoy the fishing, clamming, beach-combing and boating that highlight western peninsula outdoor activities.

Not all Kenai Peninsula recreation revolves around the region's natural splendor; man-made events also contribute to the Kenai's reputation as a playground. Each community offers its share of good time, but a few of the events have gained statewide and even national recognition.

Several communities have fishing derbies, Seward has its Mount Marathon race each July, and Polar Bear Jumpoff Festival in January. Moose Pass residents gather at the ballpark at summer solstice. Each May Cooper Landing residents work off spring fever in a five-mile Snail-A-Thon along Snug Harbor road. Pledges for the participants are donated to community projects. Soldotna has Progress Days in July and rodeos in summer, the York Winter Games in January and the Alaska State Championship Sled Dog Races in February. Kenai welcomes the Christmas holidays with a Family Affair built around the Christmas tree lighting. The Tustumena 200 Sled Dog Race draws mushers to Clam Gulch in January and February. This small community is home to 1984 Iditarod Trail Sled Dog Race champion Dean Osmar. Happy Valley hosts a Fourth of July rodeo, and each August fair-goers gather at Ninilchik for the Kenai Peninsula State Fair. Seldovia has a renowned Fourth of July celebration chock-full of games and activities including a greased pole climb, penny hunt, parade, and an outdoor barbecue so tasty that townsfolk and visitors line up along Main Street for more than a block.

Homer, cultural queen of the peninsula's communities, seems to have enough events to satisfy just about anyone's whim. In recent years the town's artists, performers and entrepreneurs have supported events from a Spring Arts Festival to fishing derbies. The Kachemak Bay Shorebird Festival celebrates the spring arrival of thousands of shorebirds migrating to breeding grounds in western and northern Alaska. The Homer Society of Natural History, operating through the Pratt Museum, sponsors topnotch lectures and exhibits. The Center for Alaskan Coastal Studies offers beach walks and environmental education

A familiar and often welcome sight to Seward Highway travelers is Summit Lake Lodge, about 20 miles south of Turnagain Pass. The lodge and its restaurant are open year-round on the north shore of Summit Lake. The area's deep snow, routinely exceeding 12 feet, makes it a popular winter playground for skiers and snow machiners. (Michael DeYoung)

LEFT: *Fishermen cast for grayling in Lower Fuller Lake and Dolly Varden in Upper Fuller Lake, both reached from a trail into the Kenai Mountains north of the Sterling Highway. The trail, initially quite steep, levels out into a valley in the Mystery Hills, where there are beavers, game birds, raptors and memorable views of the Kenai River valley. (Ron Levy)*

ABOVE: *The telltale scallops of skiers mark the snow of the Chugach National Forest in late winter. The national forest embraces 1.9 million acres of the eastern peninsula, excluding state and private inholdings. (Cliff Riedinger)*

opportunities. Theater fans look forward to performances by Pier One Theater or Fresh Produce, an alternative group. For those with an eye to the casual, public radio station KBBI's Concert on the Lawn has just the right ambiance.

Residents and visitors to the Kenai enjoy the best of many worlds: a vigorous economy, developing social, cultural and athletic opportunities and a natural playground among the most spectacular in Alaska.

Bibliography

Barry, Mary J. *A History of Mining on the Kenai Peninsula.* Anchorage: Alaska Northwest Publishing Co., 1973.

___ *Seward Alaska, A History of the Gateway City, Vol. I: Prehistory to 1914.* Anchorage: MJP Barry, 1986.

___ *Seward Alaska, A History of the Gateway City, Vol. II: 1914-1923, The Raildroad Construction Years.* Anchorage: MJP Barry, 1993.

Bendock, Terry. "It's Wake-Up Time on the Kenai River," *Alaska's Wildlife*, Vol. 25, No. 3. Juneau: Alaska Dept. Fish and Game, May/June 1993.

Bernton, Hal. "Get out of the way…Clem Tillion does what he thinks is best," *Anchorage Daily News*, Aug. 23, 1992.

Betts, Robert C.; Christopher B. Wooley; Charles M. Mobley; James C. Haggarty; Aron Crowell. *Site Protection and Oil Spill Treatment at SEL-188.* Exxon Shipping Company and Exxon Company, USA, 1991

Grundman, Donna and Don Ohr. *A Place Called Hope.* Hope, Alaska, 1986.

Hornaday, James C., ed. *The Native, Russian and American Experiences Of The Kenai Area Of Alaska.* Kenai, Alaska: Conference on Kenai Area History, 1974.

Kenai Peninsula Borough Coastal Management Program. Soldotna: Kenai Peninsula Borough, June 1990.

Kenai River Comprehensive Management Plan. Anchorage: Alaska Dept. of Natural Resources with Kenai Peninsula Borough, Soldotna, November 1986.

Kizzia, Tom. "Living life on Homer's historic homestead, homesteader to preserve past for future," *Anchorage Daily News*, April 1, 1990.

Lehner, Devony, edit. *Kenai River Landowner's Guide.* Homer, Alaska: Kenai Soil and Water Conservation District and U.S. Dept. of Agriculture, Soil Conservation Service, December 1992.

Morgan, Albert Weldon "Jack." Unpublished manuscript, "Memories of Old Sunrise." Edited by Rolfe G. Buzzell.

Nielson, Jonathan M. *Armed Forces On A Northern Frontier.* Westport, Conn.: Greenwood Press, 1988.

Pedersen, Walt and Elsa. *A Larger History of the Kenai Peninsula.* Sterling, Alaska: Walt and Elsa Pedersen, 1983.

Stallings, Mike. *Index to the Seward Gateway, A Newspaper 1904-1910.* Seward: Seward Community Library, 1983.

Strohmeyer, John. *Extreme Conditions.* New York: Simon & Schuster, 1993.

Whittaker, Doug and Bo Shelby, PhD. *Kenai River Carrying Capacity Study, Important Findings and Implications for Management.* Alaska Dept. of Natural Resources, Division of Parks and Outdoor Recreation, October 1993.

Where Is Yakataga?

By William Wakeland

Editor's note: *A 47-year resident of Alaska, William Wakeland is a free-lance photographer-writer living in Anchorage.*

On a map of Alaska, Cape Yakataga juts into the North Pacific some 40 miles west of Icy Bay, which is near Mount St. Elias. Two miles west of the cape is a Federal Aviation Administration airstrip of World War II vintage. In 1948 a U.S. Geological Survey team, of which I was a member, set out to find where this airstrip was. The location was to have been the terminus of a survey westward from Icy Bay to provide base data for contour maps. But the "known" points for the contours had vanished.

We learned that the latitude on existing charts placed this airstrip one and one-half miles out to sea. This knowledge came through many painstaking hours of stellar observations in coordination with time signals in Greenwich Mean time. From that rather jury-rigged start, we moved eastward, using now outdated methods under conditions of extreme weather and terrain. Helicopters and laser instruments would have cut months off our time, even starting from established points. But we

William Wakeland, member of a 1948 survey crew, pulls a dog cart on a hard sand beach. Early prospectors used the carts, pulled by dogs, to haul their gear along the Yakataga beach. (Courtesy of William Wakeland)

got the job done and had a great adventure on one of the last of the surveys done the hard way.

Our leader, Joel Langhofer, now a long-retired veteran of many surveys — some of them in Alaska — lives in Denver, where the USGS still produces the maps. Joel's assistant, Les Ganahl, a photogrammetric engineer, was also from Denver. This was his first field trip. I held status as an "Alaska Sourdough," having homesteaded on Kachemak Bay two years earlier. Sam Pees, Neal Barbin and Joe Campbell were all college students, with varying temperaments, soon to have

nicknames best not revealed here.

We had flown to Yakataga from Cordova, where we had left the Alaska Steamship Co. vessel *Aleutian* late in May, and used quarters provided by the FAA personnel. Joel had traveled to Icy Bay to try to locate monuments placed in the 1920s by a hydro-graphic survey team. Finding that tidal and glacial action had obliterated these monuments, he returned to order additional equipment and figure out how to meet this unexpected challenge. To establish a base line and begin the survey, he first had to find where we were.

We soon met all six of the people then living beyond the Yakataga airstrip eastward to Icy Bay, a distance of about 25 miles. Four of them lived at the cape, where there was a post office, and two lived way to the east at Little River. These two, Jack Carson and Carl Killion, were of immense help to us. They helped solve our transport problem by providing carts that we pulled on the beach, carts with big wheels and long, skinny poles used to guide them from behind while dogs pulled them from the front. We pulled them from the rear, using the poles like a tongue, minus the dogs.

Jack and Carl had established several cabins along the beach from which they sluiced for beach gold. They offered the cabins to us to store our gear and to get out of our tents occasionally.

As we progressed eastward from the airstrip, Joel had his hands full, coping with lousy weather, logistics, crossings of swift rivers, deciding who was the cook for the day, mosquitoes and thick underbrush. Fire partially destroyed one tent, and a bear messed up another one. In addition, four of us were greenhorns to the wilds of Alaska, or anywhere else for that matter.

The first task of the actual survey work was erecting signals along the beach and selected high points in the foothills of the Robinson Mountains. From these points, theodolite and plane table observations were made to tie the points together by triangulation, and to show distance and elevation to other points that might be discernible on aerial photos. Sounds simple enough, doesn't it?

Early in the morning on the next promising-looking day, we'd leave camp early and climb all day to reach a signal on a mountain, carrying the instruments, tripods, plane table, rifles, etc., only to have a little fog blow in, or the beach haze thicken to where we could not find the signals down below. So we'd retreat to await another day, and that might be in several days. And this describes what was a good day.

Joe Campbell erects a signal on Three Sisters Mountain. (William Wakeland)

Often four or five of us had to be up in the mountains because the earth was so unstable that we had to position ourselves to rotate the instrument through a circle with no one moving, not even to swat a mosquito.

While finding a way to a mountaintop was often challenging, at least we could do it in poor weather, as long as we could see enough to erect a pole with a flag in the right spot. Another task that could be done on bad days was moving along the beach.

Walking the beach, whether with a cart, packboard or instruments, was often a search for hard sand, and our tracks weaved back and forth like those of a drunk. However, we did have other motives at times. Along the beach were all sorts of interesting things, like rocks and fossils. We would often have to empty collections from our pockets and start all over

again. And there were gulls, seals — we even saw a land otter loping along once — and weird shapes of dried kelp.

The little band of land between the high tide line and the mountains broadened as we progressed eastward from White River, and more small streams, meandering sloughs and broad tidal flats harbored more life. Nature's bounty was welcome as we ran low on

food. Three kinds of salmon, silvers, pinks and chum could be kicked out of shallow places in the streams. By August we were eating geese, ducks and garden produce from Carl and Jack.

While running a traverse to find distance, direction and elevation up Johnson Creek, we came across what may have been among the first oil wells in Alaska. It was a small derrick, with a noxious outflow on the ground. Carl told us this operation dated from 1923. Equipment had been hauled in by tractor from a dock in Icy Bay, crossing Big River on a cable bridge. While some oil was found, the dock was soon washed away, and the only evidence visible to us, in addition to the derrick, was part of a deadman anchor for the bridge. In fact, according to Carl, the dock had been located two miles out from where the beach is now. Apparently massive changes are

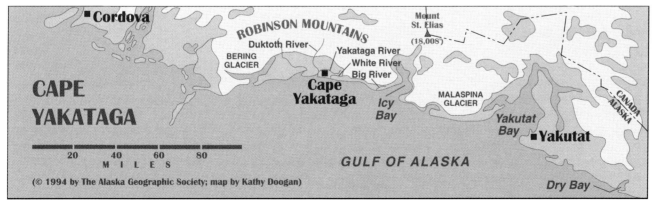

CAPE YAKATAGA

Cordova

ROBINSON MOUNTAINS

Duktoth River
Yakataga River
BERING GLACIER
White River
Big River
Cape Yakataga

Mount St. Elias (18,008')

CANADA ALASKA

Icy Bay

MALASPINA GLACIER

Yakutat Bay
Yakutat

GULF OF ALASKA

Dry Bay

20 40 60 80
MILES

(© 1994 by The Alaska Geographic Society; map by Kathy Doogan)

ABOVE: *Crew chief Joel Langhofer looks over this scene of Guyot Bay and the Robinson Mountains near Icy Cape. (William Wakeland)*

LEFT: *An oil derrick built about 1923 on Johnson Creek commemorates early oil exploration along the Yakataga coast. (William Wakeland)*

occurring as Guyot Glacier recedes.

Early in September, Joe and Sam had to leave for college. The weather was turning and we were running out of time. Fighting wind, rain, high tides, ice on the beach and treacherous Clay Point, we did manage to finish the survey at Carson Creek, well into Icy Bay.

On October 1, during a lull in a particularly foul stretch of weather, a bush pilot from Cordova, flying for famed pilot Mudhole Smith, plucked us and our gear off the beach and flew us to the airstrip in five trips. The wind was so strong his little Piper Cub was airborne in 80 feet. Next day we were in Cordova, enjoying warm baths, restaurant meals and reminiscing at the Alaskan Hotel Bar.

What has happened since 1948 to the domain of Jack and Carl? I was planning to return until inquiries proved the old saying: You can't go home again.

Jim McAllister, the state's Regional Forester at Juneau, briefed me on the history of the area since statehood. And I picked up a copy of the Public Review Draft of the Yakataga Area Plan from Project Manager Nancy Pease.

The 273-page report covers the area from Cape Suckling east to Dry Bay, southeast of Yakutat. The area of our survey is about one-fourth of the total shoreline.

The state selected much of this area from the federal domain under the statehood act. It has been logged since about 1969. The principal dock for the logging is near Carson Creek in Icy Bay, and a road system extends well to the west. A large part of this more level portion is now designated Mental Health Lands, set aside to fund mental health care in Alaska, and is out of state control.

Another road from Yakataga airstrip extends east and up the White River nearly to the glacier, to serve a placer mining operation. During the 1950s and 1960s, extensive oil exploration, both onshore and offshore, accounted for roads and drill sites shown on current maps. The entire area looks like a jigsaw puzzle on the proposed classification map.

To my surprise, moose have moved in. We never saw any in 1948, and figured the bears, both black and brown, were responsible.

Carl and Jack are now long gone, and would no longer want to live there. But our map-making notes have sure been put to use. And, thank goodness, Yakataga airstrip is back on dry land.

The Worth of a Birch

by George Matz

Editor's note: *Anchorage resident George Matz works in the energy and environmental field, and in 1994 is consulting on sustainable forestry.*

Birch are the cornucopia of the boreal forest, furnishing the forest with an abundance of benefits that helps sustain a variety of fauna and flora. The boreal forest would not be the same ecologically, economically or spiritually, without the bounty and beauty of birch.

Birch provides a diversity of benefits throughout its lifespan, starting with a tiny seed. It is fortunate that birch yield an abundance of seeds since the future of an individual seed is not good. Many are culled and few are chosen to complete the cycle and become a mature tree. But the birch seed that we will follow is so destined.

This tree started out as a tiny spring flower nestled in the catkin of an old birch, high on a hillside overlooking the Tanana River. The old tree was one of the few birch still left on the southeast slope of the hill that now has been mostly covered with white spruce. Last summer, on a hot afternoon, a lightning bolt ignited a tinder dry black spruce on the north side of the hill. A wildfire started, quickly spread, skipped over the ridge and torched several acres of white spruce near the old birch, but it was untouched.

A worker strings plastic tubing among birch trees to collect sap for Original Alaska Birch Syrup Co. of Fairbanks. When daytime temperatures are above freezing and nighttime temperatures below freezing, the sap starts to run. Gravity draws the sap downward to a central collection point. (Jeff Weltzin)

As spring turned to summer, the flower became a seed, a tiny nutlet with two wings. Then, on a breezy day in late fall, the seed twirled down from its dangling catkin and landed in a snowy opening where the fire had reduced the majestic white spruce to sticks of charcoal and the mossy groundcover to bare soil.

This is an ideal place for the birch seed to settle. Ash from the burnt vegetation will provide the essential nutrients needed by the seed when it germinates. Also, the thick loess deposits on the hillside are well drained and free of permafrost. But most of all, now that the ground will not be shaded by spruce, the birch will have good exposure to the radiant energy of the sun.

Spring comes with a frenzy. The temporary vacuum created by last summer's fire quickly fills in with fireweed, horsetail and other pioneer species, establishing the first successional stage (moss-herb) after the fire. Our birch seed, now a seedling, has to compete for survival along with about a million other birch seeds for every acre of burn. The competition for sunlight and nutrients is severe and most seedlings fade away.

A few years later, our favorite birch seedling has grown into a tall sapling. This second successional stage (tall shrub-sapling) is reached about the same time that the local population of snowshoe hares begins to recover from its crash just previous to the fire. The sweet inner bark of deciduous saplings is a favorite source of food for the snowshoe hare. The expanding population of hares nibbles away at the birch saplings that cover this part of the hillside. Again, many trees do not survive.

The sapling we are following also survives the onslaught of numerous moose that now inhabit the area. During winter, moose survive by browsing on the twigs of birch, willow and other deciduous trees, severely damaging some of them. Moose also snap in two some saplings, bent over with snow, while attempting to feed on the upper branches that tend to be more palatable.

Birch saplings are more than fodder for herbivores. In earlier times, indigenous dwellers of the boreal forest considered birch saplings an essential material for winter transportation. Clarence Alexander, a Gwich'in from Fort Yukon, says that the strength and flexibility of birch made excellent frames for snowshoes, which gave Athabaskan hunters mobility to hunt and trap successfully during the winter. Birch was also used for making bows and sleds.

Three Decades Later

It is now about 30 years after the fire and the next successional stage (dense tree) begins. An even-aged stand of birch, all having germinated immediately after the fire, now dominates the forest on this patch of hillside.

Viewers on the other side of the river can witness the beauty of birch. The ever-white streaks of birch trunks add contrast to the spreading evergreen boughs of white spruce spared by the fire. The crown of the birch grove adds color that changes with the season. The leaves burst into a vibrant green in the spring, age to a darker green in the summer and then turn radiant gold in the fall. Even in winter, birch adds color to the forest; its brown buds becoming redder with the approach of spring.

The leafy crown of the birch tree also adds to the ecology of the forest. The closed canopy of the birch stand shades the forest floor, hindering the growth of herbs, shrubs and even its own seedlings. But the shade is not as limiting to the white spruce seedlings, slowly growing beneath the birch, that will once again dominate the hillside. It will be nearly a century, however, before the white spruce will succeed birch as the dominant species.

In addition to shade, the crown produces seed and litter. The birch we are observing reaches its most productive age for seed-bearing at 40 to 70 years. Although the amount of seed production varies

RIGHT: *Unsawed trees and stacks of finished lumber await handling at Bob Zackel's lumber yard in Fairbanks. Zackel manufactures tongue-and-groove paneling, and prefers using trees that are 40 to 60 years old with a diameter of 10 inches to 14 inches. Older trees develop heart rot that weakens the wood, making it unsuitable for sawing. (George Matz)*

FAR RIGHT: *Clarence Alexander from Fort Yukon shows three pairs of snowshoes. Athabaskans from the Interior fashioned snowshoes, baskets and other items necessary for their daily chores from birch wood or bark. The snowshoes on the left with the wider mesh were made recently; the other two pair are from an earlier time. (George Matz)*

from year to year, each summer our tree produces about 15 pounds dry weight of catkins that contain about 9 million seeds.

Both catkins and seeds provide an important source of food for birds. Ruffed grouse feed on the catkins. Birch disperse their seed in the fall and winter when redpolls, pine siskins, chickadees, and other songbirds need an abundance of food to survive the cold winter. A stand of birch in the Interior can have an annual seedfall of 72,800 seeds per square meter. By contrast, seed production by the next most prolific tree, white spruce, is only 4,000 seeds per square meter.

Besides seeds, the birch canopy litters the forest floor with leaves. When shed in the fall, the litter smothers moss growth that cools the soil. The litterfall from a stand

of birch will typically weigh from 1.8 to 3.6 tons per acre, more than any other tree in the boreal forest. The decomposition of this litter adds nutrients, such as calcium, magnesium and phosphorus, to the soil. Slower-growing white spruce will use these nutrients. Once again, our birch serves as a provider for another species, even its successor.

Other forest life thrives on the birch itself. Porcupines will girdle the bark off the trunks and branches of birch. Beavers, from the slough next to the wide bend in the river, will waddle up the slope to take the juicy birch, branch by branch, to the water below.

Commercial Harvest

Forty-five years after the fire, the next successional stage emerges.

The birch stand is now considered a hardwood forest. Our favorite tree is nearly 70 feet tall and 12 inches in diameter at breast height.

It is during this successional stage that hardwoods like birch have their greatest commercial value. Steve Clautice of the Alaska Division of Forestry in Fairbanks says that about half the commercial timber volume of the Interior consists of hardwoods. "Birch is the most significant hardwood tree," he adds. "Birch makes up about two-thirds of the hardwood volume and aspen about a third."

Commercial value can be obtained from living trees. Entrepreneurs in the Anchorage and Fairbanks area have turned an old practice into a new Alaska product, birch syrup.

Every spring for the past few years, Jeff Weltzin has been tapping about 10,000 birch trees on 720 acres in the hills above

Fairbanks. He says, "the tree has to be at least 40 years old to produce enough sap." He finds "those 60 to 80 years old seem to produce the most sap."

A mature birch tree will produce about a gallon of sap per day. Peak flow conditions will last 10 to 14 days. This will boil down to two or three eight-ounce bottles of tasty syrup that in late 1993 sold for $8.50 apiece. Birch can be tapped year after year making it a good example of sustainable development.

Live birch also provides bark. Athabaskans used birch bark to make canoes and baskets for every-day use. They still make plenty of birch baskets that are now sold as Native handicrafts, larger ones selling for more than $100 a basket.

In Alaska, the most common use of harvested birch is firewood. Considered the best firewood in the Interior, birch yields about 18.2 million Btu's for every cord of dry wood. Steve Clautice estimates that the annual current demand for firewood in just the Tanana Valley area is about 15,000 cords, half being birch.

Bob Zackel in Fairbanks contends that firewood is not the best use of prime birch. Owner of Alaska Birch Works, Bob prefers to use birch for manufacturing tongue and groove paneling. Instead of getting $100 a cord for firewood, Bob says "I can get $1,200 to $1,400 for an equivalent amount of birch."

John Manthei, owner of Custom Woodworking in Fairbanks, makes quality birch furniture and cabinets. He advises that "birch has to be used with discretion."

Although its grain has sensuous curves, too much of it can create a confusing pattern for some people. Nevertheless, John believes "there is good potential for utilizing Interior birch providing it is cut selectively because of the low percentage of high quality trees typical to the Interior forest." This means low volumes that favor operations that are able to get more value-added income from a tree.

Another user of prime birch trees is The Great Alaska Bowl Co. in Fairbanks. Using a 22-step process, the company makes wooden bowls out of 14-inch blocks of wood. Marti Steury, company president, says they can make up to 54 sets of bowls (four bowls per set) from a 32-foot log with a 14-inch diameter. A complete set sells for $129. Marti estimates that the economic value added to a log this size will be at least $4,000, which doesn't include turning rejects into byproducts, such as bird feeders, or the value added by several artists who use the bowls as their media.

Birch has a wide range of economic value to Alaskans.

FAR LEFT: *Marti Steury, president of The Great Alaska Bowl Co., and her associates went to Granville, Vt., to get the blueprints for the cutting machine that creates the birch bowls. The machine was originally designed in 1855, when birch bowls and furniture were common, and it took three and one-half years for a machine to be built and refined before manufacture of finished bowls could begin in Fairbanks. Steury opened for business in August 1991, and the company has since made more than 40,000 bowls. (George Matz)*

LEFT: *This display at The Great Alaska Bowl Co. illustrates the steps in making bowls from birch. Finished products line the top two shelves. The third shelf shows the initial block of wood and the beginning cuts. A birch block 14 inches or larger in diameter with a moisture content of 40 percent to 60 percent is ideal. Several concentric bowls of different sizes are made from the same piece of wood. First the smallest bowl is made, then the next largest, until all the wood is used. If a bowl breaks, it then becomes material for a bird feeder. Nothing is wasted. Even the sawdust residue from the sanding reappears in sculptures by a local artist. (George Matz)*

In this mixed stand of birch and white spruce, the tree on the left has bracket fungi on its trunk, often a sign of heart rot. As the birch begin to die out, the growth rate of the white spruce accelerates, and eventually this species dominates the forest. (George Matz)

Looking at the options that exist with one large tree having few defects, making birch syrup will yield about $20 worth of product per year. This is nearly as much as if the birch were harvested and sold as firewood which would bring in about $25 (it takes at least four large birch trees to make a cord of wood). If this tree were made into paneling, however, it would be worth about $300 or more. But the biggest money-maker is birch bowls, which have a value greater than $4,000 a tree.

The Dilemma

It is now 1994, 61 years after the fire. Our birch tree is now facing a new dilemma. Although it has been a survivor in the natural world, its fate may be decided by an alien process. The Alaska Department of Natural Resources, Division of Forestry, which now manages the land where our birch tree resides, has included this area in its "Five Year Forest Operations Schedule" for the Tanana Valley. Released in June 1993, this draft plan initially proposed large-scale logging on 80,000 acres of boreal forest, starting in 1994 and lasting 10 to 20 years.

Like the forest itself, however, forest management seems to go through periods of change. The intensive management that was favored just a few years ago by foresters seems to be transforming into what is now called "ecosystem management," where value is given to all species, not just those having the greatest commercial value.

And just as a species survives by adapting to the conditions it is faced with, so does an agency. Partially because of strong public opposition to the five-year plan, the Division of Forestry announced in October 1993 that any large-scale logging in the Tanana Valley will be delayed until 1997. Meanwhile, they plan a more thorough inventory of forest resources.

BIRCH

Birch trees (genus *Betula*) are not exclusive to the boreal forest, but these vast conifer/hardwood forests, which circumscribe the northern latitudes of the world, are most closely associated with birch.

Of the 40 some species of birch that exist in North America, Europe and Asia, only three species are found in Alaska. Two of these species, dwarf arctic birch and resin birch, are stunted shrubs that grow in muskeg, tundra or alpine slopes where few, if any, trees are able to obtain the nutrients necessary for growth. The other species, paper birch, is a medium-sized tree found in the northern forests of North America from Newfoundland to Alaska.

Paper birch has several geographical varieties. According to *Alaska Trees and Shrubs* (1972) by Leslie Viereck and Elbert Little, three varieties found in Alaska's spruce-hardwood forests are: Alaska paper birch common to the forests of the Interior and Southcentral, Kenai birch found mostly in the Cook Inlet region and Western paper birch that extends into some of the large river valleys of Southeast that have headwaters in the Yukon or British Columbia. Where ranges overlap, these varieties will hybridize. In fact, even dwarf birch and resin birch will hybridize with paper birch.

If left to contending just with the forces of nature, our birch tree will continue to grow for a few more decades. Growth will then yield to decay and spires of white spruce will soon dominate the hillside. Heart rot will inflict the old birch, creating good opportunities for woodpeckers to drill out nesting cavities. An unusually strong wind will eventually sweep through the forest and the weakened tree will topple.

Even then, it will still provide. The birch's rotting trunk, lying on the ground, provides nutrients for plants and creates habitat for a diverse array of small animals.

Whatever evolves in the next few years will not only determine the fate of our birch tree, but the future of Alaska's boreal forest. Will large-scale clearcutting on many of the hills around Fairbanks leave bare flanks for the next few decades? Or will most of the boreal forest remain intact and continue to provide a diversity of ecological, economic and aesthetic benefits?

By Lyn Kidder

Editor's note: *A former resident of Sitka, Lyn has previously written about that city's raptor rehabilitation center for* Alaska Geographic®

Eating From the Land in Southeast

At the foot of mist-shrouded mountains, on the shores of green islands set in gray seas, the Native people of Southeast have lived for centuries. The area's wealth of natural resources allowed the Tlingit, Haida and Tsimshian to develop a rich, complex culture. Many of the methods of using the foods that Nature provides so plentifully in season are still practiced today.

Winter brings the rain and snow that nourishes this abundance. By March and April the sprouts of salmonberry, goosetongue, fiddle-head ferns and beach greens can be eaten.

Eulachon, also called hooligan or candlefish, move up Southeast rivers, usually in March or April. The pencil-thin fish are caught with gillnets or large dipnets. The fish are rendered into oil, a process that traditionally was done in large bentwood boxes and small canoes, but in modern times is accomplished with pressure cookers. The eulachon's excessive oiliness gave it the name "candlefish," and they can be wicked and lit like a candle.

Also in April herring spawn. To collect the spawn, hemlock boughs are placed at the low tide line and anchored with rocks. The herring eggs, like clumps of tiny, white beads, stick to the hemlock. The

Natives hold onto the sticks and dip the eggs into boiling water for a few minutes to cook them until slightly crunchy. Before widespread use of the modern freezer, the eggs were simply eaten off the boughs, perhaps with some seal oil, or air-dried for storage and later rehydrated. Today, various recipes for herring egg salad are shared at potlucks.

Herring eggs can also be harvested on seaweed, either hair

Salmon, a staple for early Tlingits of Southeast, hang to dry at a camp north of Sitka where youngsters are taught traditional ways of handling foods. (Frederic Moras)

kelp called *ne* or macrocystis kelp called *daaw*. The latter was so popular with the Japanese that they were overharvested, and since the 1970s commercial harvest has been banned. There are,

however, two commercial spawn on kelp in pound fisheries near Craig and Hoonah. In this fishery, large bags of webbing are hung from floating, wooden-framed pens, and the kelp and herring are put inside. The herring are released after they have spawned, and the kelp is harvested, salted and sold, mostly to the Japanese market.

In May, the first growth of black seaweed can be harvested, although it is hard to pick since it is still short. The traditional method for preserving black seaweed is to pack it in wooden molds and allow it to dry into a brick. Crunchy and salty, it tastes a bit like popcorn and can be eaten as a snack or used in cooking.

May is also the time to collect gull eggs. A rich source of protein, they are available for only a few weeks. The gregarious birds nest in colonies, and while old-timers patiently listen to each egg and leave the ones in which they hear a chick, other people take no chances, setting aside all the eggs in an area and returning the next day to collect the fresh ones.

Summer is the season of plenty in Southeast. Four species of salmon, king, red, chum and pink, course the region's waterways. The fish are smoked and canned, but the bulk are frozen. As late as the 1950s, most salmon were dried. "We used to dry it, completely dry," remembers Herman Davis Sr. of Sitka. "First we'd soak it in brine. My dad used to have a big, wooden barrel. He used to fill it with salt water and put in a potato with a tenpenny nail stuck in it, and it would sink. Then he'd keep adding more salt until it floated, and that's when he knew there was enough salt to preserve the fish."

Silver salmon eggs, left in their membranous sac, are soaked in brine and placed in the smokehouse for a few days. Salmon eggs can also be fermented, but "you've maybe got to grow up tasting it," laughs Davis. "It makes a kind of cheese. During World War II, the military personnel (stationed in Sitka) used to watch for my boat to get some from me. It's good with crackers and beer." Called *kahaakw ka s'eex* in Tlingit, the fermenting is done in glass jars, "no plastic and no metal," Davis' wife, Vida, cautions. "People do it improperly, and that's how you get botulism." There's a side benefit to developing a taste for fermented salmon eggs. "If you have any parasites or worms in your system, the salmon eggs are going to drive them right out. Cleans out your system for the whole year. No kidding," said Davis.

Many Alaskans, Native and non-Native, have smokehouses, mostly homemade affairs. The essentials of a smokehouse are an enclosed space, a wood stove with a pipe leading into the enclosure and racks on which to hang the fish or meat. In Southeast the wood of choice is alder, a fast-growing tree. Purists remove the bark from wood that is to be burned during the first hours of smoking, claiming that the bark

Billy Haynes (left), Anthony Morino and Edward Littlefield show off beach peas they collected at the NATIVE Fish Camp. (Frederic Moras)

imparts a bitter taste to the food.

Halibut can be fished as early as February, though they are in deep water at that time of the year. In July and August, the halibut follow and feed on pink salmon as they return upstream to spawn, and then the halibut can be fished from shore. "My grandfather would bait a halibut hook and put it out a ways from shore, with a seal bladder tied on as buoy. When he saw it bob down and disappear, then he knew he'd caught it," remembers Davis. The halibut is dried in thin strips in the sun, making halibut jerky.

Berries grow abundantly in

Southeast: salmonberries, blueberries, huckleberries, thimbleberries and elderberries. Historically they were dried, but today those that are not immediately eaten are frozen. Charlie Joseph, who died in 1986 at age 97, told his daughter, Ethel Makinen, of an old method of preserving berries. A ring of tree bark would be carefully removed from the trunk. The ring was placed on a flat rock over the fire, and a mixture of water and berries was poured in. More berries and water were added during several days, and the thick jelly that formed was perhaps the first fruit leather.

John Littlefield, right, instructs Ricky Urias in how to cut a salmon to prepare it for drying. (Frederic Moras)

Summer also brings beach peas, a tiny version of the domestic pea, and greens such as goosetongue continue to be available. As the season advances, the greens are steamed or sauteed with butter and garlic, rather than eaten raw.

As autumn approaches, the focus turns from fishing to hunting. Sitka black-tailed deer, which move to lower elevations as snow accumulates on the mountainsides, are hunted. All of the deer meat is used, and is either frozen or dried into jerky for storage. The tongue is boiled and eaten like a sausage. The brains are used in tanning the hide, which can then be made into moccasins. The antlers are used to make handles for knives and other implements, and the hooves and dew claws are crafted into ceremonial rattles and regalia. If one family or individual is known for using a certain part of the deer, successful hunters will try to save that part for them.

Harbor seals are hunted in October, when the pups are grown and the seals are fat from their summer feeding. Some hunters wait until the seals are feeding on mollusks rather than fish, which they claim gives a fishy taste to the meat. Seals have a thick layer of fat just below the skin. The oil from this fat, liquid at room temperature, has a slightly fishy taste and was once used as a preservative for meat, fish and berries, but is now used as a condiment.

Fall is also the time to harvest Indian rice, or black lily, a plant that grows along the shores. The grains, produced only during the plant's second year, cling to the roots, and the entire plant must be uprooted to harvest the rice. Care must be taken not to overharvest, and Indian rice is now eaten as a delicacy.

Knowledge of traditional Native foods and how to harvest and prepare them is passed on through several cultural programs in Southeast. Ray Nielsen Jr. is the coordinator of the Sitka Tribe of Alaska's Subsistence Foods Program. The program's purpose is to ensure survival of traditional gathering and preparation methods of Native foods. The program emphasizes working with elders and youth, preserving the knowledge of the former and sharpening the skills of the latter. Individuals and businesses support the program through donations.

"Some fishermen donate a portion of their salable product to us, and we can give them a receipt for income tax deduction," said Nielsen. The foods prepared through the program are donated to the Senior Center, to home-bound elders, disabled individuals and to youth groups who use some of the prepared foods for fund-raisers. The preparation of foods for elders and those who are unable to do it for themselves is a long-standing Tlingit tradition.

"Nothing was ever wasted," remembers Ethel Makinen. "Every part had a use." For example, salmon heads were fermented, and were called "stinky heads." "Long ago people used to make them in wooden barrels. Things used to come in the barrels, things like butter or flour. Otherwise you could bury them in burlap sacks, at very low tide." Another method of making stinky heads is to bury the heads between layers of huge skunk cabbage leaves. The tides wash over them for at least five days. The heads are then dug up, washed and eaten, with the cheeks being the best part.

John and Roby Littlefield contribute to the preservation of the subsistence lifestyle with the NATIVE Fish Camp they operate each summer for children of Sitka, both Native and non-Native. NATIVE stands for North American Traditional Indian Values, and the goal is to teach some of these values. The children, ages 6 to 16, camp in the woods at Dog Point, a few miles north of Sitka. John Littlefield's family has used this fish camp for generations. "I was younger than these kids when I first started coming out here," said John. "We'd spend practically the whole summer here."

The children catch and smoke salmon, and gather berries and other wild edibles. Meals consist mostly of foods that they have prepared.

"Subsistence is putting food on the table," summarized Ray Nielsen Jr. "It is the lifestyle of those who choose to enjoy the abundant resources that Nature provides. It is not a way of life, but rather a part of life."

Rocky Stone: Holding Her Course Toward Art

By Ann Chandonnet

Editor's note: *Ann is a free-lance writer who lives in the Anchorage area.*

Whether she lives by the Atlantic or the Pacific, fabric artist Rocky Stone keeps her eye on the slow and steady: the water, the rock, the sky.

Stone grew up in the Atlantic seaside town of Gloucester, Mass.; now she lives in the similarly small, similarly fishing-oriented town of Cordova. On her living room wall is a painting of a famous Gloucester statue, "The Man at the Wheel," a fisherman in a slicker not unlike a Cordova bronze by a local sculptor that stands at the small boat harbor.

"He has been my inspiration because he 'holds his course,'" says Stone, a creative woman for whom the best small talk is art talk and inspiration talk.

Stone first came to Alaska in 1966. She fished springs and summers on salmon seiners and then spent winters in Colorado. She made Cordova, population 2,800, her year-round home in 1980, the first summer she worked in a cannery.

"You really appreciate being in the open air on a boat after you have been in a cannery," she comments, wrinkling her nose to emphasize the contrast.

She escaped the cannery for the seiner again, soon graduating from deckhand to navigator and running the deck. She still does some gill-netting every season.

Fishing has been a part of Rocky Stone's life since she first came to Alaska in 1966. Here she is aboard the seiner Gail T. *out of Cordova. (Simone Nolan)*

"I'm driven to do my [artistic] work, but fishing is my mainstay economically," Stone explains, "because at this point in time I can't make a living with my work."

Two awards that Stone received in 1993 may help her to make the jump to full-time artist. One was a prestigious Juror's Choice Award from Anchorage; the second was fourth place from a show in Fairbanks.

Juror's Choice Awards and their attendant publicity bring an artist to the notice of the public, sometimes for the first time, and also justify the artist's charging more than a minimal wage for the hours put into the art.

Stone's Juror's Choice Award grew out of the fact that three of her quilted pieces were accepted into the Earth, Fire and Fiber show at the Anchorage Museum of History and Art. The show opened in January 1993, and later moved to Fairbanks and Juneau.

"This show was a big step forward for me," Stone says.

"What a day that was when they called me," she adds excitedly. "We lived without a phone for so many years that we take it off the wall at 5:00 every night and listen to classical music and just be happy. Because Sully was out, I forgot to unplug the phone, and it rang at 7:00. [Sully is Rocky's long-time companion.] It was Kathy Vail-Roche, co-chairman of the exhibit, and she congratulated me, and I said, 'You mean you accepted one of my kimonos?' because I had had a hard time getting my entries to Anchorage on time. The plane had passed us by two days in a row because of bad weather."

"And she said, 'No, no; we've accepted all four that you submitted.' It was hard for me to believe. Then when she said I had the Juror's Award, I hit the ceiling in the kitchen. I thought she was kidding; I was so floored."

A subtle, abstract kimono titled "Bass Rocks" received the Juror's Award. "It's done in a crazy quilt technique that I fell in love with and then learned," Stone explains.

Like Bass Rocks, many of her quilted kimonos have titles that derive from scenes of water, seaside resorts, sloughs

BELOW: *With this kimono, called "Frank Lloyd Wright's Window," Rocky Stone won second place at the Ketchikan Arts and Crafts Guild Exhibition. The artist used the Italian bargello technique to create an image reminiscent of Wright's architectural prairie. Wright often designed windows with long, narrow panes of clear glass accented with small colored glass inserts in chevrons or squares. (Rocky Stone)*

RIGHT: *The design on this kimono, "Ed King's Yard," recalls the yard of long-time Cordova resident, Ed King. Artist Rocky Stone explains her attachment to this image: "I've always wanted to capture the feeling I get from that yard, when all the flowers are blooming. So I made a kimono with massive color that suggests flowers in bloom and flowers gone to seed. It's a tribute to how the beauty of his yard is such a nourishment to my soul." (Simone Nolan)*

in the Cordova area or gardens. The other three accepted for the show were "Cabo San Lucas," executed on a blue background with yellow and red the primary colors; "The Gardens at Marblehead," on purple with red and green the primary colors, a portrait of two flowerbeds bordering a central staircase; and "Barcelona," on a black background with gold, teals and red its primary hues.

The Juror's Award not only meant acceptance and praise from the art world for Rocky Stone; it also meant $1,000.

"Sully and I flew over to the show and went out to eat at the Crow's Nest and had a really nice bed and breakfast and blew the whole thing," says Stone gleefully.

Stone has been putting sewing machine and needle through their paces since she was a preteen. "I would make my wardrobe," she recalls. "And even then my color choices were considered unusual. People would say, 'Blue and green don't go together.' And I'd get comments like, 'You're not going out in that outfit, are you?'

"As soon as I had a home of my own, I wanted a sewing machine. I've had this machine now since 1980, and I consider it an old friend."

The wearable art that is earning Stone a growing reputation for excellence in design and execution did not surface until about 1988. "I used to do applique and embroidery work of Prince William Sound," she explains. "Then we had the *Exxon Valdez* oil spill and everything changed for me. I reference everything in my work in terms of the oil spill. Then when a needlework teacher visited from Seattle, I took a class in bargello and adopted that technique. I decided to apply it to kimonos, and make the back like a painting in fabric. What makes bargello special for me is the dividers, the quilted troughs or "rows"; they make all the colors come alive."

Traditionally, bargello refers to an Italian needlepoint technique in which stitches are arranged on the canvas so that they form rows at an angle to each other. "I use bargello as an arrangement of bands of colors to form chevrons or V's," Stone explains.

Her bargello is related in form to what some quilters call strip quilting. But the effect, as Stone uses it, is totally different, because there is no assembly into squares or repetitive patterns such as baby blocks, stairsteps or log cabins.

Stone likes to integrate an active physical life with her contemplative, artistic pursuits. Often she hikes the steep trails of the mountains around Cordova. Vacations outside Alaska may include some muscle-bending rock climbing in Joshua Tree National Monument. And later, there'll be a kimono called "Joshua Tree," inspired by that place.

When she's uncertain about the progress of her work or encounters a dry spell, Stone gets together with other Cordova artists. "Pat McGuire is one of my encouragements," she says. "When I have a blockade…, I go to her and talk it through. Or I go to [sculptor] Joan Jackson."

Combining deep purple with green or scintillating teal with scarlet is still at the forefront of Stone's stubborn, idiosyncratic artistic consciousness. "What I get off on is testing the limits of color combinations," is the way she puts it. "I like purple and red together, for instance. I remember being told as a kid, 'Blue and green should never

be seen.' 'Purple and red, I'd rather be dead.' Sayings like this are part of your upbringing; it's hard to throw over all that."

Although pieced quilting in king, queen and crib sizes is a major craft movement in the nation at present, Stone is unmoved. "Real quilts never got me too excited, because it was too much to hold in your lap or run through your machine."

One year, she admits with a sigh, she succumbed to producing six or seven wall hangings that are the size of futon throws. "But I could see right away when making them that what I wanted was some kind of small palette."

She sees her "kimono," a thigh-length jacket with roomy sleeves, as analogous to the haiku: something restricted in size but not in scope; a minimal container that can hold a great deal. This is her chosen canvas, and

Stone can do a great deal with it.

"Haiku, brush painting, Japan itself — they all interest me," Stone says. "Keeping in that context felt natural to me." She has never been to Japan, but hopes to visit some day.

Her first kimono was "Bearskin Neck," named after a small strip of land on the Massachusetts seacoast where legend has it that an early colonist killed a bear. What was once wilderness and bears is now cozy cottages and narrow streets, so Stone's design portrays an abstract view through a lowered window into a flower garden.

Stone lives in a tiny frame cottage overlooking Cordova's small boat harbor and the canneries where she once labored. Guests must trudge up 120 unpainted wooden steps, past another house and into a slope of dripping evergreens, to reach her front door, where rufous hummingbirds whir in the damp, ferny foliage, and sip red syrup from a feeder she has placed outside a living room window to attract them.

In case guests don't catch Stone at home, there's a mailbox at the top of the staircase where messages can be left.

In her entry hall, dried gingko leaves and flamingo feathers share a wooden bowl. Piles of linoleum blocks reflect another art form she embraces.

In the quiet living room, a fringed and beaded bag and paintings by other

artists adorn the walls. In the tiny, adjoining sewing room, the ironing board is always up, and a bulletin board holds fabric samples and drawings for future designs. A kimono with the design bordered in an apple green jade color is in the works.

Stone may occasionally use satin or gold lame in her fiber creations, but she steers away from pastels, chintzes and neons. Generally she uses 100 percent cotton, and silk. Occasionally she mixes in brocade and beads.

Slim, dark-haired Stone goes about her fabric art as many poets go about writing poems: "Sometimes I have the name first. Sometimes the name comes to me as I'm working. But if I have a concept, the effect first, it never works. I have to play with the fabrics. They grow on me. I know the colors and get those together, but then it kind of takes its own form and shape."

"Your work is the accumulation of all your personal history," Stone feels. "From each experience, you grow into the next. I will be halfway into a kimono, working with it, and the colors in it will trigger the next combination in my brain and I will run quick and write it down. It's just a thrill, like fireworks going off."

Although fame has been slow in arriving and fortune is well behind, joy is in good supply for Stone. "I love working on things early in the morning and I think, 'Oh, if only everybody could be as happy as I am right now.' Work is everything," she says earnestly. "If you can't be happy when you are working, you have missed so much. It is wonderful to find something that means so much and lose yourself in it. So many people search and search, and they don't understand: it's in the work."

Wales and Anchorage Residents Aid Spectacled Eider

By Connie M.J. Barclay

Editor's note: Connie Barclay works in the public affairs office of U.S. Fish and Wildlife Service in Anchorage.

An injured sea duck currently protected under the Endangered Species Act was rescued near the tip of the Seward Peninsula in western Alaska in January and flown to Anchorage to be cared for by the Arctic Animal Hospital.

The young female spectacled eider is recovering thanks to the efforts of Native villagers, a bush helicopter pilot, a National Park Service biologist, an airlines flight crew, biologists with the U.S. Fish and Wildlife Service (USFWS) and an Anchorage veterinary clinic.

On Jan. 5, Wales resident Vincent Okpealuk noticed a lone bird perched on a snow drift. The bird seemed oblivious to snow machines buzzing around it.

"At first I thought she was resting before moving on," Okpealuk said. Upon closer investigation, he determined the duck was an injured female spectacled eider unable to fly. He immediately called the U.S. Fish and Wildlife Service office in Anchorage and asked what to do.

"I knew that she was on the Federal Endangered Species List and I wasn't sure if I should approach her," Okpealuk said.

"We used to see lots of spectacled eiders many years ago, but their numbers have dwindled alarmingly over the years."

Following instructions from USFWS biologists, Okpealuk placed the eider in a cardboard box. "She was weak and quite sick acting," he said. "She just kept tucking her head under her wings and hiding."

Afraid the bird wouldn't survive the night, Okpealuk located an Evergreen Helicopter pilot who flew the bird to Nome where an Alaska Airlines crew took over care, escorting the eider to Anchorage. Once here, the bird was transferred to USFWS endangered species biologist Ginny Moran, who took her to Arctic Animal Hospital, where the bird was placed in the care of wildlife veterinarian Dan Mulcahy of the Bird Treatment and Learning Center.

"We're . . . excited to be able to help this rare bird," Mulcahy said. He determined the bird had a broken wing and suffered from

USFWS endangered species specialist Ginny Moran examines Opal, an injured female spectacled eider rescued from the village of Wales by Vincent Okpealuk. (USFWS)

dehydration. "She's eating and swimming in the freshwater tank now," he added.

According to Moran, caretakers named the spectacled eider Opal after Okpealuk, and chances are good for a full recovery.

Populations of the spectacled eider, an arctic sea duck that sports a distinctive white eye patch, have been declining rapidly on its primary breeding grounds on Alaska's west coast, leading the U.S. Fish and Wildlife Service to list the species as "threatened" under the Endangered Species Act on May 10, 1993.

USFWS biologists estimate that breeding birds on the Yukon-Kuskokwim delta declined from 50,000 or more pairs in the early 1970s to current numbers of a few thousand pairs.

So far, causes for the decline have not been identified. Researchers do not know for sure where spectacled eiders spend most of their lives. After brief summers breeding on Alaskan and Russian tundra, they migrate to unidentified wintering areas on the Bering Sea and surrounding coastal areas.

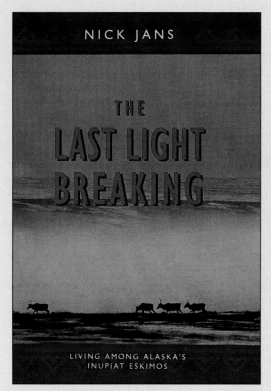

NICK JANS

THE LAST LIGHT BREAKING

LIVING AMONG ALASKA'S
INUPIAT ESKIMOS

The Last Light Breaking,
by Nick Jans, Alaska Northwest
Books, an imprint of Graphic
Arts Center Publishing Co.,
Portland, Ore., 224 pages, no
illustrations, 1 map, notes on
sources, suggested reading list,
no index, hardcover, $21.95.

"Few places are broad enough
to bear the weight of our dreams;
the Brooks is one of them." So
writes Nick Jans in this carefully
crafted, gently told series of
essays about life in the northwestern Arctic, in the Kobuk and
Noatak river valleys.
The presence of the
mountains is always
there in the book,
sometimes in the
background, sometimes
at dead center. And in
the valleys among the
peaks, the Inupiat
Eskimos fashioned a
culture, one based on
natural rhythms. The
beat of these rhythms
and his gradual
understanding of the
tune lies at the heart of
Jans' book.

After a float trip
down the Kobuk River
with a friend, Jans on
a whim signed on as
storekeeper at the
trading post in the
Eskimo village of
Ambler. His initiation into life
at Ambler was somewhat
problematic. "Except for the
pilot I was the only white face,
but everyone seemed friendly
as I stepped into the bright
August sun.
"Are you the new teacher?"
A big man smiles, holding out
his hand.
"No. The new store manager,"
I replied, smiling back and
holding out mine.
"Ambler Trading?" His mouth
tightened, and the big man
turned his back.

"Suddenly no one else was
smiling either, and I was left
wondering where to put my
hand.... I stuffed the empty hand
into a pocket and pretended to
watch the pilot unloading
freight. Actually, I was eyeing
the distance between me and the
plane door. But my pack was
already in the truck, and I was
broke anyway, five thousand
miles from home. I scrambled
over the pickup's tailgate.
"Five bucks, white man." The
big man held out his hand again,
this time palm up. 'If you work
for that German, you pay.'
"I could tell it was no use
explaining that Erik was Dutch.
As I trudged down the hill with
my pack, eating the pickup's
dust, I had the feeling that I'd
just started to pay.
"Thirteen years later,
thumbing through my journals,
I wonder what kept me from
jumping back on that plane.
Twenty-four years old, barely
three months in Alaska, I was
as alone as I've ever been — 50
miles above the arctic circle, 200
miles from the nearest road,
and it had taken me less than a
minute in town to get the bum's
rush."

With any adaptation to a new
home comes a few misadven-
tures. Ambler residents were
prone to sporadically firing their
guns for a variety of reasons, or
sometimes no reason. And as
Jans writes, "One evening I
added my two cents to the
general mayhem. I was sitting
alone, cleaning rifles after a
hunt.... I'd checked them all first,
of course, and emptied each
magazine. Maybe I was tired, or
maybe it was the Jack Daniels I
was nipping, but when I picked
up Erik's .30-06 Sauer carbine...
and casually squeezed the trigger,
it erupted in my hands. Somehow
I'd missed the last bullet.
"I sat openmouthed, staring at
the dark hole I'd punched in the
closet door. Behind that door was
the town's phone relay, twenty
thousand dollars' worth of
electronics. The bullet...had
missed it by an inch, plowed on
through the wall into the adjacent
clinic, two feet over the heads of a
visiting doctor and his wife...and
disappeared out the far wall.
They accepted my stumbling
apology, but there was nothing I
could say to the small crowd of
grim-faced villagers who'd come
running. I'd just joined the
Accidental Discharge Club, and
they didn't let me forget it for
months. Not only was I Erik's
cousin, but an idiot and a menace
to society."
Jans survived his initiation and
blended into the lifestyle of his
new home, first as a storekeeper
and later as a teacher. His new
home was new itself. Ambler was
"founded in 1958, by far the
youngest of eleven villages in the

region, and one of the youngest in the state. Following a bitter political feud, six families from Shungnak had banded together to start their own village. The site they chose, twenty-five miles to the west, was a rich one — good places for gillnets, plenty of firewood, and fine hunting; twice a year, the tundra around town was awash in waves of migrating caribou. And so the new village of *Ivisaappaat*, officially known as Ambler, had grown and prospered, a community of proud, independent people — independent, at times, to the point of anarchy."

Survival for the people of the Kobuk and Noatak revolves around a seemingly unending round of fishing, hunting and gathering. Most of Jans' essays center on these subsistence activities: Minnie Gray filling her seine net with whitefish, Clarence Wood hunting caribou at Onion Portage or shooting a wolverine from his snow machine. Again, Wood shooting a wolf, and with unspoken challenge urging Jans to do the same. At times, Jans' words betray his uncertainty. He sees the beauty and spirit of wild, free-ranging animals, but he knows that the Natives see nothing wrong in killing the wildlife. Jans honors the wolf alive; Wood honors it dead.

But there are lighter moments, when the search for food and clothing takes a second seat...to basketball. "Beat 'em, Bust 'em, that's our custom...." Basketball is taken seriously by the residents of the northwest Arctic. Jans' stint as coach of the Noatak Lynx showed him just how seriously. "When you figure that there are eight small villages in the Northwest Arctic Borough School District with basketball teams, and that each school plays between ten and twenty regular season games, two per trip, you get an idea of the expense — and that's just travel. Not counting the buildings, the yearly cost for the school district's basketball program — coaches, uniforms, equipment, travel — is well over a hundred thousand dollars. The People want basketball that badly. The residents of Ambler, when asked for input on the design of their new school, specified that a gym was first on the list, and they got what they asked for: a basketball floor with cramped classrooms tacked on as an apparent afterthought."

Eskimo narratives introduce each chapter, insights into the Native lifestyle of the Kobuk and Noatak in their own tongue. These words, and those of Jans', blend to create a moving painting of life among the mountains and along the rivers, places that handily bear the weight of Nick Jans' dreams.

—*Penny Rennick*

S H A R I N G

Recollections of the Serum Run to Nome

Mr. Tony Polet was the mayor of Nome at the time of the epidemic during which the famous dash with the serum was made. He was also my landlord during the years 1951 and 1952, his daughter Mrs. Boucher a good friend. It was hard not to have anyone in the town not your friend in those days due to the small population and the close quarters during the winter.

[I was talking with Mr. Polet about the serum run], and he told me his side of the serum controversy. This is what I thought you would find interesting....

He told me the epidemic was all but over when the idea of the serum started. I think he told me the main center of the epidemic had been in a small community just to the west of Nome and it had not been a real bother in the town of Nome. He told me he was able to send a radio message ...and in this message he said the serum was not needed and to not try to get any to them. But, he said, the newspapers were making a big thing of it and there was no stopping them.

Every now and then I will hear someone talk about the heroic dash to Nome and I sort of chuckle. But, I have seldom told of my conversation with Mr. Polet because the serum dash is indeed a wonderful story and I think, why spoil it.

I was in Alaska about 11 years in Nome, Aniak, Kotzebue, Summit and have lots of stories, mostly about bush flying. I am sure it will not surprise you to hear I was with the CAA. Most of us in those years with the CAA were ex-GIs and got our training in the service in WWII. I had been a Marine, all branches were represented.

One of my greatest pleasures in my 74th year of life is the *Alaska Geographic*®. I am in my 13th year of reading it and enjoy and learn with each issue.

—*Raymond F. Hawk*
Edmonds, Wash.

ALASKA GEOGRAPHIC Newsletter

Penny Rennick / **EDITOR**

Kathy Doogan / **PRODUCTION DIRECTOR**

L.J. Campbell / **STAFF WRITER**

Vickie Staples / **CIRCULATION/DATABASE MANAGER**

Pattey Parker / **MARKETING MANAGER**

Index

Photographers

ALASKA GEOGRAPHIC. Back Issues

The North Slope, Vol. 1, No. 1. Charter issue. Out of print.

One Man's Wilderness, Vol. 1, No. 2. Out of print.

Admiralty…Island in Contention, Vol. 1, No. 3. $7.50.

Fisheries of the North Pacific, Vol. 1, No. 4. Out of print.

Alaska-Yukon Wild Flowers Guide, Vol. 2, No. 1. Out of print.

Richard Harrington's Yukon, Vol. 2, No. 2. Out of print.

Prince William Sound, Vol. 2, No. 3. Out of print.

Yakutat: The Turbulent Crescent, Vol. 2, No. 4. Out of print.

Glacier Bay: Old Ice, New Land, Vol. 3, No. 1. Out of print.

The Land: Eye of the Storm, Vol. 3, No. 2. Out of print.

Richard Harrington's Antarctic, Vol. 3, No. 3. $12.95.

The Silver Years, Vol. 3, No. 4. $17.95.

Alaska's Volcanoes: Northern Link In the Ring of Fire, Vol. 4, No. 1. Out of print.

The Brooks Range, Vol. 4, No. 2. Out of print.

Kodiak: Island of Change, Vol. 4, No. 3. Out of print.

Wilderness Proposals, Vol. 4, No. 4. Out of print.

Cook Inlet Country, Vol. 5, No. 1. Out of print.

Southeast: Alaska's Panhandle, Vol. 5, No. 2. Out of print.

Bristol Bay Basin, Vol. 5, No. 3. Out of print.

Alaska Whales and Whaling, Vol. 5, No. 4. $19.95.

Yukon-Kuskokwim Delta, Vol. 6, No. 1. Out of print.

Aurora Borealis, Vol. 6, No. 2. Out of stock.

Alaska's Native People, Vol. 6, No. 3. $24.95.

The Stikine River, Vol. 6, No. 4. $15.95.

Alaska's Great Interior, Vol. 7, No. 1. $17.95.

Photographic Geography of Alaska, Vol. 7, No. 2. Out of print.

The Aleutians, Vol. 7, No. 3. Out of print.

Klondike Lost, Vol. 7, No. 4. Out of print.

Wrangell-Saint Elias, Vol. 8, No. 1. $19.95.

Alaska Mammals, Vol. 8, No. 2. Out of print.

The Kotzebue Basin, Vol. 8, No. 3. $15.95.

Alaska National Interest Lands, Vol. 8, No. 4. $17.95.

Alaska's Glaciers, Vol. 9, No. 1. Revised 1993. $19.95.

Sitka and Its Ocean/Island World, Vol. 9, No. 2. Out of print.

Islands of the Seals: The Pribilofs, Vol. 9, No. 3. $15.95.

Alaska's Oil/Gas & Minerals Industry, Vol. 9, No. 4. $15.95.

Adventure Roads North, Vol. 10, No. 1. $17.95.

Anchorage and the Cook Inlet Basin, Vol. 10, No. 2. $17.95.

Alaska's Salmon Fisheries, Vol. 10, No. 3. $15.95.

Up the Koyukuk, Vol. 10, No. 4. $17.95.

Nome: City of the Golden Beaches, Vol. 11, No. 1. $15.95.

Alaska's Farms and Gardens, Vol. 11, No. 2. $15.95.

Chilkat River Valley, Vol. 11, No. 3. $15.95.

Alaska Steam, Vol. 11, No. 4. $15.95.

Northwest Territories, Vol. 12, No. 1. $17.95.

Alaska's Forest Resources, Vol. 12, No. 2. $16.95.

Alaska Native Arts and Crafts, Vol. 12, No. 3. $19.95.

Our Arctic Year, Vol. 12, No. 4. $15.95.

Where Mountains Meet the Sea: Alaska's Gulf Coast, Vol. 13, No. 1. $17.95.

Backcountry Alaska, Vol. 13, No. 2. $17.95.

British Columbia's Coast, Vol. 13, No. 3. $17.95.

Lake Clark/Lake Iliamna Country, Vol. 13, No. 4. Out of print.

Dogs of the North, Vol. 14, No. 1. $17.95.

South/Southeast Alaska, Vol. 14, No. 2. Out of print.

Alaska's Seward Peninsula, Vol. 14, No. 3. $15.95.

The Upper Yukon Basin, Vol. 14, No. 4. $17.95.

Glacier Bay: Icy Wilderness, Vol. 15, No. 1. Out of print.

Dawson City, Vol. 15, No. 2. $15.95.

Denali, Vol. 15, No. 3. $16.95. Out of print.

The Kuskokwim River, Vol. 15, No. 4. $17.95.

Katmai Country, Vol. 16, No. 1. $17.95.

North Slope Now, Vol. 16, No. 2. $15.95.

The Tanana Basin, Vol. 16, No. 3. $17.95.

The Copper Trail, Vol. 16, No. 4. $17.95.

The Nushagak Basin, Vol. 17, No. 1. $17.95.

Juneau, Vol. 17, No. 2. Out of print.

The Middle Yukon River, Vol. 17, No. 3. $17.95.

The Lower Yukon River, Vol. 17, No. 4. $17.95.

Alaska's Weather, Vol. 18, No. 1. $17.95.

Alaska's Volcanoes, Vol. 18, No. 2. $17.95.

Admiralty Island: Fortress of the Bears, Vol. 18, No. 3. $17.95.

Unalaska/Dutch Harbor, Vol. 18, No. 4. $17.95.

Skagway: A Legacy of Gold, Vol. 19, No. 1. $18.95.

ALASKA: The Great Land, Vol. 19, No. 2. $18.95.

Kodiak, Vol. 19, No. 3. $18.95.

Alaska's Railroads, Vol. 19, No. 4. $18.95.

Prince William Sound, Vol. 20, No. 1. $18.95.

Southeast Alaska, Vol. 20, No. 2. $19.95.

Arctic National Wildlife Refuge, Vol. 20, No. 3. $18.95.

Alaska's Bears, Vol. 20, No. 4. $18.95.

The Alaska Peninsula, Vol. 21, No. 1. $19.95.

ALL PRICES SUBJECT TO CHANGE

Your $39 membership in The Alaska Geographic Society includes four subsequent issues of *ALASKA GEOGRAPHIC®*, the Society's official quarterly. Please add $10 for non-U.S. memberships.

Additional membership information is available on request. Single copies of the *ALASKA GEOGRAPHIC®* back issues are also available. When ordering, please make payments in U.S. funds and add $2.00 postage/handling per copy for Book Rate; $4.00 per copy for Priority Mail. Non-U.S. postage extra. Free catalog available. To order back issues send your check or money order or credit card information (including expiration date and daytime telephone number) and volumes desired to:

The Alaska Geographic Society

P.O. Box 93370-KPI
Anchorage, AK 99509-3370

NEXT ISSUE: *People of Alaska*, Vol. 21, No. 3. It is said that the land shapes its people. In Alaska it is just as true that the people shape the land. This issue looks at some of the remarkable people who made Alaska what it is, not necessarily politicians or well-known people, but folks living the Alaska lifestyle. To members 1994, with index. Price $19.95.